BROKEN

The Life and Times of Erik Daniels

As told by...

Terry Austin

Broken: The Life and Times of Erik Daniels

Published by Austin Brothers Publishing
ISBN - 978-0-9983071-9-0

Broken is based on real life experiences. Some names, characters, places, and incidents are changed at times to protect the privacy of certain individuals.

Printed in the United States

"My grandmother always told me that she believed I was an angel from heaven. I never really believed it, but when you look back, I should be dead, more than dead. I should be in prison, but I'm not. I don't know if God really had something, and I was too stupid to ever follow it or what, but my Grandmother was convinced God had some huge plan I was supposed to fill, and then she died, and I messed it all up and who would ever use me for anything..."

Contents

Broken

I've never understood why, but broken people have frequently been attracted to me like a thirsty dog is drawn to a puddle of rainwater. Perhaps it's because I'm in a wheelchair and people naturally assume I must be broken as well, that maybe I will understand them better than others. However, I don't think that's the only reason because sometimes it even happens before people know I'm crippled.

I just typed the word "crippled," and it caused me to think that being crippled might be the reason for some. Crippled people have a compulsion to be around other crippled people. Like they say, "Birds of a feather..."

Yet, as I said, not every broken person drawn to me has known that I'm crippled. Besides, personally, as a crippled person, I'm not drawn to other crippled people. To be honest, I don't like to be cast among the handicapped. When I neared seminary graduation, well-intentioned friends and others tried to point me in the direction of counseling, thinking it would be a good outlet for me in ministry without the physically demanding duties of preaching and pastoring a church.

But that wasn't for me. The seminary even set up an appointment for me to visit a place called Warm Springs in Georgia, to interview for a chaplain position. You might have heard of Warm Springs. It's the place where FDR went for therapy to treat his polio when he was President. Although polio is no longer a plague faced by many, the facility now treats people with all kinds of paralyzing maladies.

I traveled south to visit the place, took the tour, and even sat for the interview, all the while knowing this was not for me. I'm not comfortable around people in wheelchairs. Although I'm not well-versed in the psychological arts, I think I know the reason. I don't like to be considered "one of them." I understand their condition and know first-hand the difficulties they face, but I don't want to be labeled as one of them.

I rambled on about all of this because I want to make the point that crippled people are not necessarily attracted to other crippled people. I don't think that's why so many broken people have found their way into my life. There has to be another reason.

Let me add that when I say "broken," I don't mean crippled. Some of the broken that I reference have had some kind of physical malady, but for most of them it's more of a social awkwardness, or a history of bad behavior, or something else that makes them an outcast.

There have been many of them during my six and a half decades. Even as a kid, for some reason the kids that no one else liked wanted to be my friend. It wasn't always easy to know what to do, and to be honest, I didn't always respond the right way.

One of the most painful episodes in my life is one of those memories which still produces embarrassment, even though it happened fifty years ago. The incident transpired in a musty church basement which was the home of our youth Sunday School class.

My friend Steve had arrived early, and we were discussing the activities from the previous week. Steve was a good friend, mainly because he and I were always at every church event. Steve and I had very little in common. We attended different schools and lived several miles apart. His father was a leader in the church where my father was the pastor.

Steve and I did share our music—we both loved to sing. We were allowed to join the adult choir, probably because they were in need of tenors. When we got warmed up, Steve and I could drown out the entire choir with our high-pitched resonant tones.

Outside of the choir, Steve and I didn't share many common interests, but we were still friends at church. Perhaps it was a shared tragedy which had united us. Steve was not much bigger than me, but one Sunday night he was carrying me down the stairs at church. Three steps from the bottom, he tripped, and we both tumbled. The wall at the foot of the steps broke our fall and my collarbone. The broken bone was painful, but Steve suffered even more.

My bone mended and his spirits lifted, and we became closer friends. We both had the ability to overlook our differences and concentrate on our similarities. I did not condemn him for his lack of interest in baseball. I enjoyed visiting his house, even though he often ended up in a fist fight with one of his four brothers. We shared many good times, but few of them remain in my memory today.

The Sunday morning that sticks so firmly in my recollection involved Steve and a girl named Sandy. I don't really recall much about Sandy other than what occurred on this fateful Sunday. She was one of those kids who just appeared at church, without any family or friends. Looking back from my adult perspective, I realize that she was probably looking for someone to care for her.

If I remember correctly, Sandy was a tad bit heavy and several inches taller than me (but who wasn't; the tallest I ever stood on my crutches was 5'4"). She had shoulder length hair that flipped up on the end, which was the popular trend of the day. Sandy walked into the classroom where Steve and I were goofing off before the majority of kids arrived. Steve and I were minding our own business, probably laughing about something mundane. Sandy walked over to us and spoke, but her attention seemed singularly focused on me. I'm not normally self-conscious, but for some reason, she made me uncomfortable.

After exchanging our meaningless greetings, she stretched out her hand which had been tucked behind her back. In her grasp was a brightly wrapped gift, which she stuck in my face. It was one of the few times in my life when I was nearly speechless, but I did manage to mumble something unrecognizable.

Sandy responded, "This is for you."

It was summertime. Therefore, I knew immediately it was not my birthday, so I stammered, "What for?"

Her words almost knocked me unconscious. "Just because I like you," she said.

As she was speaking these words, it seemed as if the entire church youth group walked through the door. I was on the verge of facing one of the most awkward situations of my life—everyone hearing how an unpopular girl liked me. I would never hear the end of this. Making quick decisions during a crisis has always been one of my strengths, and this time was no exception. I immediately discerned that no one except my friend Steve had witnessed this transaction. Without even examining the present, I quickly handed it to Steve and said, "Here, you can have this!"

Being unaware of my discomfort, Steve was just glad to get a present. He immediately tore away the wrapping paper and uncovered a bottle of cheap aftershave. Neither one of us was old enough to shave, but he splashed some on his face like an experienced barber.

My initial reaction was to breathe a sigh of relief because it seemed that no one noticed my embarrassment. However, I then began to think about Sandy. By the time I looked up, she had walked away and taken a seat in the back of the room.

I don't remember ever feeling so shameful. For some reason, Sandy had come to believe that I was someone who might care about her. Almost in desperation, she had reached out for my friendship only to be rejected once again. Within a few weeks, Sandy quit coming to church, and I have never seen her again.

As I said, this experience still haunts me today, fifty years later. Perhaps that memory is what attracts the broken to me. I find it difficult to turn people away. Whenever someone catches my eye, I tend to acknowledge them in some way—a nod, smile, wave, or a spoken word. I think it was Sandy who taught me the importance of always leaving the door open to continued conversation and relationship, even when the gap between you is enormous. I remember the shame of that Sunday morning and have no desire to experience it once again.

Sandy was not especially repulsive in appearance. Neither did she have an overbearing personality nor any disgusting traits. The only thing unacceptable about Sandy was her dissimilarity. For some reason, she did not fit in with us normal kids. For a fifteen-year-old boy, this is an obstacle the size of Mt. Everest.

She didn't have what we considered a normal family with a father and mother who participated in her life. Sandy was obviously from a lower social class than most of us, and she just did not meet our expectations. She was different.

Sandy was not the first broken person to find a place in my life, nor was she the last. I remember a kid named Troy in grade school. The teacher refused to allow him to push my wheelchair. He had a propensity to throw temper fits, and she feared he might get mad and roll me down a steep hill next to the playground.

In High School, there was Louis whose mother was a professional wrestler, and Carl who played the trumpet next to me in band. Others are still around, so I'll not mention their names lest they're not aware I considered them broken back then. It continued through college and seminary. My wife could easily describe Clay and C.J. and a handful of others whom we have reminisced about over the years—wondering whatever happened to them.

However, the attraction didn't stop once I graduated and entered the world of adulthood. There was Jose, a farm worker, an illegal immigrant who latched on to our family. He came to our house to teach Sharon how to make tortillas and chili Rellenos. Jose occasionally disappeared for months, or even a couple of years at a time. But he always came back. He called one day from the airport in Amarillo, seventy-five miles away, and wanted me to come get him. I did, of course. Drove him up to Kansas where he had a job and then heard later he beat up his wife/girlfriend (I'm not sure which) and went back to Mexico. Jose even got me thrown out of a funeral once, but that's a story for another day.

Another young man who was hired to work on a farm in our community became a part of our family. He was just a poor country boy with no family and nothing to his name. We took him in, fed him occasionally. He even babysat for us a time or two, so we could have an evening out. He returned to Oklahoma where he was from and was promptly arrested on an outstanding warrant. We heard that shortly after getting to jail, he broke out with the chicken pox that he apparently caught from our boys a week earlier.

The list of people like this is long, and I remember more of them each time I travel down this particular memory lane. People who were often discarded by others, sometimes considered untouchable by some, and frequently excluded from friendship by most. Somehow, they made it into my life and usually into our home.

I know I have stretched Sharon far beyond her comfort level with some who have come knocking on our door. I have to tell you that I'm extremely proud when I see some of this same trait in my sons. Some people like to pick up stray dogs and cats. It seems that I am more in the stray people business.

I've wandered a far piece from the question of why broken people are attracted to me so let me take another stab at it. I hesitate offering this suggestion because I don't want to propose there is something admirable about me. I'm just a guy with the same struggles and fears that other people possess. In fact, to be honest, the reason for the attraction of others has nothing to do with anything I have ever done or have the ability to do. It is an inherited trait, like my blue eyes.

I don't know what it is but for some reason people like me. It is an innate skill. The reason I say that is because I saw it clearly in my father. When Daddy walked in a room, there was just something about him that communicated, "This is a guy you want to know." He wasn't gregarious or especially social. In fact, he once told me that he would rather sit in a corner by himself than be in the middle of a group of people. I can identify with that.

But Daddy taught me something else, and my mother pitched in with this as well. They stressed the importance of always giving preference to other people. Let them have first choice, step out of the way if they're coming through, renounce your spot if it's where they want to be, lend a hand when someone is in need, and always speak kind words. I learned it, and it is a part of how I live. Again, that's not something I take credit for any more than a jockey's son would take credit for knowing how to ride a horse.

But the following pages are not about all the broken people who have graced my life. Nor do I intend to bore you with tales of great things I have done to help those who have been down and out. I'm going to tell you about a new friend. I know it is the most broken friendship I have ever had, and I would not be surprised if it is also one of the strangest friendships you have ever heard about as well.

Our relationship began when I visited a website looking for a writing job. It was a site I had viewed a few times previously but never experienced any success finding work—but it doesn't hurt to check occasionally. The way this site works is that people who need something written post information about the job. If you are a writer and think you can handle the task, then you write a response.

Most of the posted jobs are from people who are seeking writers who are cheap. I don't mean people who are spendthrifts, but those who will work for very little pay. That's not me, so most of the postings are of no interest to me. However, on this Friday afternoon, one opportunity struck me as interesting.

It might have been the brevity of the post that caught my attention. Some guy named James Fisher posted these words: "Write a tell all book." That was the complete description. Nothing about a particular subject or anything you normally saw in the job postings. However, it was categorized under the three dollar sign "Expert Level" category and a 1-3 month time frame. I can and have written a book in three months time. Since he was looking for someone to write an entire book, he must be willing to pay significantly. I responded to the ad with two short paragraphs. The first paragraph was an explanation of my experience and the second described the process I use in ghost writing.

When I have applied for work before on this site, the usual response is silence. I don't know if I'm not good enough, too over-qualified, boring, or what, but I had only received one response from previous postings. It was a job I replied to several weeks earlier. I decided to get creative and wrote a funny reply to a post just to see if anyone actually read them. Sure enough, the woman wrote back, said she liked my approach, but went on to say she already had another writer. Oh well, try again.

The next morning, I received a reply from James Fisher concerning his tell-all book. It read, *I hate trying to talk through messaging. Can you text me at xxx-xxx-xxxx so we can discuss my project.*

It was Saturday morning, and we had plans to go to our grandson's birthday party, so on the way out the door I sent him a quick text and told him I would call in the afternoon. I'll admit the thought of finding a good job floated through my mind several times that morning in the midst of the melee of a child's birthday party. I was especially curious about the "tell all" aspect of the assignment. What did he want to tell?

After lunch, I picked up my phone to call James Fisher and secure this job. If I can talk to a prospective customer on the phone, I feel confident about having success. Remember how I described that people like me for some reason. That has advantages when seeking a job assignment.

Mr. Fisher didn't answer the phone. In fact, the phone didn't even ring. It immediately went to a recording that said the phone was not available. I think that means that either the phone is turned off, out of the service area, or the bill was not paid. I was hoping for one of the first two. I tried several other times throughout the afternoon and always the same result. He already said he doesn't like messaging, and I don't like texting, but I thought I might get a response if I send a text.

I received an immediate reply.

I am in yellowstone no service for calls just texting til about 5.

Before I finished reading that message, a second came through.

Will 5000 dollars get my book wrote?

I was not ready to commit to that because five thousand might not be nearly enough for what he wanted. So I replied, asking him what he wanted and how big of a book was he expecting.

His response this time signaled the beginning of our adventure.

Well I'm 39 years old mother was a raging alcoholic sexually abused by grandfather from 12 to 14 youth group homes prison first time at 21 got out got married ran a group of skinheads til about 30 in which time (now is when I need discreet) I ordered people's deaths lots of robberies at 33 I got a new name and started my life over

At this point, James Fisher definitely had my attention. This is not the kind of stuff I normally write, but I'm fascinated with police shows on television and I love a good mystery. "Breaking Bad" was one of my favorite television shows and maybe we could spice up his story to be comparable. I'll tell you now, there was no need to spice up his story. In fact, if we want it to resemble "Breaking Bad" we may need to tone it down a bit.

For the next thirty-five minutes, we texted back and forth with negotiations about how much to pay, how to pay, and what I would do. At one point he offered a situation that included publishing the book as well as writing that was far more lucrative for me than I normally do. I told him I wouldn't accept that and countered with a better proposal for him. Perhaps that's one reason we stayed engaged; he saw I was not out to gouge him.

Once we finally settled on a price, he then wanted to negotiate about when and how to pay. That went back and forth a few times and I finally just said,

You're one of those guys who has to have the last word.

With that, we settled the deal. I was excited about the project, and I think he was happy as well.

He then wrote,

Look by the time this project is done you
will think I was the devil back then

I assured him that I was not a kid and that I could handle anything he had to say. His response:

I didn't mean it that way, I am gonna
reveal things that could put me in prison
for the rest of my life. I know your not a
kid but I know many adults who Couldn't
handle hearing about things I've done
I am asking that please don't take this
lightly. Yes we are good

He provided an email address so I could send a contract to spell out the specifics of our agreement. Then he replied with a curious statement:

I'll get that paid when I get back from the
island.

Up to that point, the only thing I knew about his location was that he mentioned being in Yellowstone where he couldn't get a phone signal. Now, there might be another Yellowstone I'm not familiar with, but I assumed that meant he was in Montana or somewhere like that. When he referenced an island, I began to wrack my brain to figure out where there might be an island anywhere near Yellowstone.

We also agreed to an extended phone conversation so he could begin recounting his story for me. I was excited to get started and was eager to hear what he had done, where he had been, and what caused him fear of future trouble. The adventure began even before our Monday conversation.

Before I could put down the phone and catch the ballgame on TV, he texted the message:

First arrest 9 years old for stealing stuffed
animals and giving them to a disabled
kid down the road I got caught because
after I took him 3 bran new in the box
flipping dog stuffed animals I have no idea
why I did it that may be the last time I
remember feeling good for anyone.

Who wouldn't be interested in this?

I confess, Saturday evening and all-day Sunday I was a little distracted by the opportunity to hear and tell the story of James Fisher. I felt like a kid whose parents promised to take him to Six Flags next week. Oh, before I go any further, when we discussed the contract spelling out our agreement, I asked what name he wanted to use. I had no idea James Fisher wasn't his real name, but I've discovered that when it comes to contracts, people sometimes want to use a company name or a legal name or something, so I've learned to ask.

He told me that his name is Erik Daniels. From that moment on, neither of us have used James Fisher again. When I initially entered his phone number on my contact list I entered it under the name James Fisher, thinking that's who he was. Now, every time he calls, the name James Fisher pops up. (I really need to change that.)

Anyway, all day Sunday I thought about Erik and his story, whatever it was going to be. I tried to reign in my imagination and not get too carried away, but I'm a writer, and I can't help but be intrigued by a good story.

Monday came around and I made a phone call to Erik. No answer once again. Left a message. Nothing happened. Several hours later I made another call—same result. At 8:30 Monday evening, I sent a text:

Erik, I tried to call today but no luck. Will you be available tomorrow?

Ten minutes later my phone beeps:

Yes I am so sorry I got horribly sick today spent all day at hospital

Wow! I'm sorry. Call me when you feel better. My schedule is flexible.

Tomorrow 1 oclock?

Works for me.

I really do apologize

Don't worry, I've been sick before so I understand.

The next day at 1:00 I sent another text. I'm assuming he is in Montana so it is actually noon for him.

Are you available today for a call?

1 thing I have yet to tell you is I have been diagnosed with liver cancer doctors have given me outside 6 months Can I put you off til 5 o'clock they are running some tests but I will be available at 5

This revelation caught me off guard, but as I previously indicated, I've always been able to think quickly. I can write a book in six months, in fact, I once wrote an entire book in one month. The funny thing is that more copies of that book were sold than everything else I have written combined. Six months would be a piece of cake.

Sure, just call when you can. I'll be ready.

I'm sorry they have admitted me again I am so sorry. I need to get on this though can we do any of it by text til I get released (hopefully tomorrow) and we can talk

Just get well!! I'm not sure how we could do anything by text. I need to hear your story from beginning to end and you would wear out your thumbs too quickly. I am aware of your urgency to get this project finished Just get to feeling better and we will make it happen.

The next day began with this conversation and progress was underway.

What time do you want to talk today?

I'm available anytime.

They are not releasing me but I can go downstairs on bench and talk to you?

Call whenever you're ready

About 11:45 on August 9th, we were finally on the phone together and I was ready to hear Erik's story. This is what I heard.

Defective

If you ever find yourself driving north out of Portland, headed toward Seattle, for most of the trip you will be able to see Mt. Rainier. It's a majestic snow-covered mass that draws tourists from around the world. Don't confuse it with Mount St. Helens; the infamous volcano to the south of Mt. Rainier. Both of these mountains are snow covered year-round and dominate the skyline in most of the Northwest. Nestled near the base of the massive Rainier is a small town that you will only see if you drive through on Highway 507. As they often say about small towns, if you blink you'll miss it.

I was born in that nondescript little village in 1978. It is not a town filled with historical markers or must-see sights. I would be surprised if any tour guide has veered off a planned route in order to present a spell-binding description of long ago tales of heroism. I have no idea who is the most famous or most important person from Rainier, Washington, but I do know it's not me. When I was young, my grandmother spoke of my entrance into the world as quite an experience for those involved. I'm not sure if that means anything coming from a grandmother. My mother's doctor had some archaic notion that labor should never be induced. He held firm to the belief that when the baby was ready to emerge, the mother's body would cooperate. When my mother was ripe and ready, she had a few cramps and some discomfort, but no labor.

The doctor, unwilling to see this as an exception to his rule, chose to wait, and wait some more. Nearly a month later he came to the conclusion that something had to be done or my mother was going to burst open like an over ripe melon left too long in the patch. With my mother in his office, and I suspect in grave discomfort, he gave the medicine to induce her labor. The only problem was that the hospital was not actually in Rainier where his office was located. She was loaded in an ambulance, and they headed toward the nearest hospital in Olympia, thirty minutes away.

As you have no doubt concluded from the first three paragraphs of my story, I survived that ordeal. I remember my Grandmother saying several times that since my birth was so unusual, there was something special about me. She talked about God having a plan for my life somehow. As you will soon discover, there was nothing else in my life to confirm those early predictions. I don't know what you believe about God, but I doubt if any theological doctrine would advocate what was to happen in my life.

Shortly after my birth, my mother and father split up, one of many marriages on her ledger–at least fourteen, as far as I know, today. It was nearly two decades later that I actually met my real father, but that's a story for later in this adventure.

You can imagine, since she squeezed at least fourteen marriages into her life, it wasn't long before my mother was remarried.

Apparently, she started dating this guy before divorce papers had even been filed on my father. The man who I called "Dad" for the first decade of my life moved in with my mom, and they shared my real father's monthly allowance from the Navy.

My real father had joined the Navy, and the plan was for my mother to connect with him shortly in San Francisco where he was stationed. From what I know now, perhaps his true plan was to find a means of getting away from her. Mom didn't want to leave the area, so she just stayed and shacked up with my stepfather. When Dad discovered she was living with this guy, he had all the justification needed, so he quickly filed for divorce, and the checks stopped coming.

I need to tell you about my childhood, and I can sum it up by simply saying it consisted of a lot of beating. Honestly, I can't remember one good moment from childhood. The years were filled with violence and constant dumb shit. During those years there were three of us boys and one girl. I didn't share the same parents with any of the others. The only thing we had in common was Mom.

Our family lived on the cusp of survival and desperation. We always had food to eat and a place to live, but it was never a well-balanced diet or a house with more than the bare essentials. My step father worked hard, but he and Mom consumed a good portion of his income via booze and cigarettes.

Mom was an especially good looking woman, which partially explains her ability to have so many husbands. Her long streaked golden hair and freckles were the ideal topping for her five-foot-nine-inch curvy body. She was still young when "liver spots," caused by her excessive drinking, began to appear on her face. Not only did she have this visible reminder of her lack of sobriety, but she always carried the smell of alcohol—always. I never thought much about it when I was a kid, but I'm sure parents, teachers, shop owners, and others in the community took a double take when she entered. The stench was strong and unmistakable. Always!

Her wardrobe consisted of nothing other than jeans and t-shirts. I never saw her in a dress, no matter the occasion. The only jewelry she wore was a wedding ring. It was tarnished and well-worn, which is not surprising because she wore the same wedding ring through all of her marriages. Whoever bought the ring to begin with must have spent a good amount because it lasted for decades and served a plethora of marriages. I never knew which man actually gave it to her, and I guess it really didn't matter to her. One other feature comes to mind, and that is she never wore makeup. I don't know if she didn't want to spend the money or if she just felt comfortable enough with her natural looks.

I'm pretty confident my mother hated me since she continually did everything she could to make my life miserable. Perhaps she loathed me because of the difficulty I caused at birth, or it might be that I was a constant reminder of my father who divorced her and cut off the monthly checks. Whenever she had the opportunity to make a decision that would affect my future, she always chose the option that was the worst for me. It began when she brought my stepfather into my life. I always called him "Richard Cranium," a nickname that somehow went over his head (if you will pardon the pun). You see, a person named "Richard" is often called

"Dick." I used "cranium" to mean "head." When you put it together, it was my secret way of calling him "Dick Head."

He was tall, which made him especially intimidating to a young child. He had spent his life working in the woods as a timber logger, and even though he was somewhat thin and wiry, his muscles were well-toned. He was no Paul Bunyan, but he was certainly powerful enough to inflict significant pain on me whenever he wanted.

His jet-black hair was a perfect match for the cheesy mustache resting on his upper lip. It always reminded me of a porn "stach." He came home from work one day with a large gash in his leg caused by a miscreant chainsaw. Although it was several inches deep, he managed to wrap the cut with his shirt and make it home. The bleeding had been stopped to a slow, steady ooze, but he needed someone to sew it up. Mom couldn't handle the blood, so she jumped into the pickup and drove to the bar, which is how she handled most of the problems and decisions of her life. He had to grab the phone and call my Grandma to come stitch him up.

His life was characterized by consistency—always wearing shirts that were made with long sleeves, but he would cut them off. You would seldom see him without a file in his pocket and a log counter hanging from a short chain attached to his shirt. The only shoes he owned were work books, usually Caulk Boots. If you're not from logging country you need to know that it's pronounced "Cork," and they are a favorite in the Northwest States and Canada, among those who work with lumber. They were made with short spikes built into the sole to make it easier to get around the soggy soil of the forest.

I grew to hate those boots because they were often used to kick me across the room. The short spikes made a grinding sound as he walked across the floor, especially after I had tracked dirt and sand in from the outside. There were countless times when I was lying on the couch, or my bed, and I heard that soft grinding sound of his heavy boots. Instinctively, I would be as quiet as a graveyard, hoping he would keep on walking past me and leave me alone. It was always better for me if he didn't notice or acknowledge my presence.

The one thing my parents did very well together was drink. They would frequently spend an evening out together by driving down to a local bar with me in the truck. They knew better than to take me inside, probably because of the fear of being turned over to authorities. Instead, they simply made me remain in the truck while they drank.

What does a kid do when you leave him alone in a vehicle? I was afraid to get out and walk home because I didn't enjoy the back of my stepfather's hand upside my cheek or his fat leather belt across my backside. So I found ways to pass the time. I would rummage through the contents of the glove box, or fish around under the seat for any stray item that might provide a distraction of some kind. Being bored was better than being beaten. It was usually dark, so most of my entertainment was limited to the imagination. Of course, the imagination of a child can be limitless, and with as much practice as I had, mine became quite active.

Sometimes they would be inside drinking for hours—I told you they were good at it. One evening while sitting in the parked truck in front of a bar, I noticed a man I didn't recognize walking toward the vehicle. I wasn't afraid. I've never been one to fear people. I stared at him as he deliberately walked straight toward the car. His pace was purposeful as if he was intent on completing a task. I looked around to see what cars might be parked nearby, but every time I turned my gaze back toward the man he made his way closer and closer. He kept looking at me as if he were deliberately walking my way. When he yanked open the driver's door, he leaned inside, looked me over for a quick second, and extended his hand holding a large plastic glass filled with water. Somehow, I'm sure my parents hadn't said anything, he knew I was in the truck by myself and how long I had been there.

I think I recall that experience because it was unusual for me to be on the receiving end of a kind gesture. He brought me a drink of water because he knew I had to be thirsty. Now that I think about it, I probably received more compassion from strangers during my childhood than from my parents.

My stepfather was mean to my brothers and sister who lived with us, but it was just meanness. He wasn't physically abusive toward them like he was toward me. For some reason, he reserved all the actual suffering for me. My grandmother said it was because of the way he felt about my Dad. Although I didn't even know my Dad at this point, he was upset because of the loss of Navy income when Dad divorced Mom. Since he couldn't take his anger out on the real culprit, I was the best target, in his thinking.

In spite of his attitude toward me, I still believed he was my father; a belief I maintained for a long time. For some reason, he did actually adopt me so legally he was my father. I think it's natural for a boy to desire to please his father and win his approval, and I was no different. It made sense that the best way to accomplish this task was to be like him. Looking back, I realize it sounds utterly stupid that I would want to please a man who was this cruel to me, but I did. That's a part of the human psyche I'll never understand.

He was a rugged outdoorsman, and like many outdoorsmen in that day, he loved to chew Copenhagen. It was rare to see him without a can in his back pocket. I studied him carefully as he pinched off a piece of the tobacco and carefully placed it inside his mouth. My mistake was not paying attention to what he did with the stuff after he put it in his mouth.

We were off on a fishing trip one afternoon and found a secluded place close to the road where we parked the truck. I was about eight-years-old at the time, and I was constantly waiting for the opportunity to do something to catch his attention and win his approval—a worthy goal.

Dad was down at the creek bed trying to catch a few fish, and I was back and forth and all around—fishing for a while, throwing rocks sometimes, aggravating my brother occasionally—generally being a kid. On one of my many trips back toward the pickup, I noticed that he had left a can of his Copenhagen on the front seat. There was nothing unusual about that, but for some reason I knew this was my opportunity. I looked around to make sure nobody, especially my Dad, was there to stop me as I climbed into the cab of the truck. Opening the can was easy even though it was still factory sealed. I knew exactly what to do since I had watched him hundreds of times. The plan was to put the stuff in my mouth and strut down to the creek. As I casually walked up to him and started a conversation, he would see how much I was like him and realize how much he loved me. What could go wrong?

You almost needed a stopwatch to time how long it took before I started feeling sick. The taste was bad enough, but then I began to feel it going all the way down my throat until it hit my stomach like a ripe watermelon dropped on an asphalt parking lot—splat. I puked all over the place. I guess the noise I made was horrifying because my stepfather came running from the creek to the truck. He quickly surmised what I had done. The open Copenhagen can was a clear giveaway.

He made me lie down in the back of the truck until I felt better. It took quite some time, but I did start to feel better; at least enough to realize I wasn't going to die. He waited patiently until I felt good enough to sit up and then he walked toward me with the can of tobacco I had already opened. He twisted open the cap and handed it to me. Then he made me eat the entire can of the nasty stuff—not just chew it up and spit it out, but swallow it.

It not only cured me of ever wanting to chew tobacco, but it also erased my desire to be like him. I gave that up as I clutched my stomach, rolling in sickness in the back of my stepfather's pickup.

The sibling I remember best is my brother, Dallas. He was Mom's son, which meant our father was mean to him, but never physically abusive. From watching our father, Dallas learned how to treat me. He was several years older and that caused me to strive hard to be close to him. Being just like your older brother is every young boy's goal.

When I was seven or eight, I was a pest. I wanted to be with him all the time. Everywhere he went, I tagged along. I got to know his friends and became familiar with his mannerisms. His likes were my likes, and his dislikes were my dislikes—except for one thing. I never understood it, but for some reason, he really disliked me. And he was mean.

Living in the country meant there was an endless supply of places to play and create problems. One of our favorites was an old barn. It was probably more like a death trap than a playhouse. Splinter filled lumber and rusty nails abounded. Inside was a pile of hay that we used as a landing spot when we jumped from the loft. I was in the loft with Dallas and his obnoxious friend, Chris Edmond, thinking I had finally arrived—I was enjoying life in the inner circle. It felt even more special when they told me I could be the first to jump from the loft into the hay.

Without a moment's hesitation, I shot toward the stairs and climbed to the top of the loft, barely touching half the rungs on the ladder. Once I was in the loft, I looked over at Dallas and Chris, and they were both shouting encouragement to jump as far as I could. I felt the excitement of being at the top of a rollercoaster just before peaking at the first climb, and I took the leap. The feeling of being suspended in air without a care in the world is only experienced by an eight-year old who feels like the most important person in the world. That feeling came to a sudden end as I crashed onto the hard wood surface below. It seems that Dallas and Chris had separated the hay, put a stack of wood in the bundle, and then re-covered the top with a thin deceptive coating. My arm was broken, but I didn't give up on striving to be my brother's best friend.

We had several Mustangs that we had adopted while living at that place. I don't mean the Ford sports car, but genuine wild horses. We kept them in the pen, and it was our job to feed and tend to their needs. One of the perks was that we got to ride them on occasion. Having the opportunity to ride horses alongside Dallas was a big treat that I took seriously.

It wasn't long after my arm had healed from the collision in the barn that I was riding one of the horses and Dallas was nearby. It wasn't unusual for him to have a BB gun since we lived in the country. We frequently carried them and shot random objects we encountered in the woods. I watched as Dallas carefully aimed one of the guns in my direction and deliberately shot the horse I was riding in the hind quarter. The horse bucked, which was too much for my little grip on the reins, and I was thrown aside like a discarded sack of trash. Now my other arm was broken.

The reason Dallas didn't stop doing things to cause me physical harm was because he had no reason to fear our parents. If I ended up with a broken bone or deep cut, it was always my fault. Once, after stabbing me in the back with an ice pick that we kept near the front door to clear the ice after a freezing rain, his punishment was to spend five minutes on the couch. I specifically remember the doctor saying, "That was really close!" All it warranted from my parents was a short stay on the couch for my brother.

The meanness and abuse from Dallas didn't stop for a long time. When I was about seventeen, my friend Scott Biller suggested that I should just stand up to him. The result was a short scuffle, but then I hit him, he fell, and I never had another issue with him. We didn't become good friends, but at least the constant abuse ended.

Dallas and I never got along. Even as adults, we never had a brotherly relationship. Though he stopped bullying and abusing me, my anger toward him seethed well into our adult years. Honestly, it didn't even stop when he died.

At that time, I had been recently incarcerated in Colorado—we'll get to that story in due course. One night after getting out of jail, I came home and found a note from my Grandmother. It was a notification that my brother had died. Later, I learned that he was killed when struck by a truck on the highway.

For some reason, I traveled to Oregon to attend his funeral. It certainly wasn't to pay my last respects. The night before the funeral, I was with some friends, and we partied hard all night long. In fact, I barely had time to rush to my motel room, take a quick shower and put on clean clothes. I didn't even have time to get some sleep before the funeral started. I arrived late to the cemetery where they were preparing to place the casket in the ground. Driving a Dodge 2500 with loud pipes, everyone heard me coming from a mile away.

A narrow gravel road wound its way into the cemetery to allow visitors to get close to the graves. As I drove down the path toward the crowd gathered near the back of the cemetery, I determined that I didn't want to park my truck on the road, so I drove onto the grass, knocking over several tombstones in the process. It was quite a sight—marble stones rolling across the lawn, sod flying in the air behind my back tires, and the loud roar of an unmuffled engine.

When the truck finally came to rest on the grass, I got out and walked toward the grave. A man, I didn't know him or who he was, tried to stop me. I just shoved him aside and said, "Get the fuck out of my way or I'll knock the shit out of you!"

All of this happened in front of my Mom, my adoptive father, my Grandmother, and other family members.

The next person to step in front of me was the preacher. I really respect that guy. He wasn't very big, but he said to me, "You're not coming in here."

"I don't believe he's fucking dead! I'm going to look," I replied.

I walked past him toward the casket. It was resting on those supports with wheels that they use to roll the casket around. It had been closed, and no one was allowed to see the body because Dallas had been disfigured in the accident. I was not deterred. I flung open the lid, and sure enough, there he was.

I don't know if it was anger or gratitude that caused me to slam the casket lid shut. But, when I did, it began to roll toward the open grave. The box didn't take a straight path into the hole, but instead, one of the rollers stuck on a dirt clod, which caused the casket to lean over sideways to the point where the entire casket fell open. The body flopped out and rolled onto the ground.

My work was finished. I arrogantly walked back to my truck and drove off. Once my wife and I were back at the motel, she was genuinely pissed, and we fought. Finally, I crashed on the bed and fell asleep. About thirty minutes later, my wife responded to a knock on the door. It was the sheriff. Someone from the funeral had reported the scene at the graveyard. He was angry and said if he could charge me with a crime he would be happy to do so. After making a few idle threats and warnings, he left.

Broken

All my life my brother had been mean to me, physically causing me pain as often as possible. The way I see it, I finally got revenge.

I have yet to tell you about the most significant experiences from my childhood years, so be prepared—things are about to get interesting.

Crushed

Living in the beautiful northwestern part of the country, in a small town, having animals and numerous places to play, along with enough siblings to keep me busy, has all the makings of a great childhood. It might sound like the ideal situation for a television series about an all-American family, finding laughter throughout and happiness at the end of each episode.

However, if it is a story about my childhood, the story would certainly not have been called *Happy Days*. I've lost count of the number of times I have been arrested during my lifetime. But I have not forgotten the first time. I was nine-years-old, and actually thought I was doing something good at the time.

We were living in a small place called Halfway, Oregon; the population couldn't have been more than 750. It was a typical Oregon town. Trees all around the place, everything was green because of the abundance of rain, and logging trucks running up and down the highway. Nothing about this town made it stand out.

Broken

There was a kid who lived down the street from us who had some kind of disease or malady. I didn't know what was wrong with him, but I remember feeling sorry for him because he couldn't walk and run like the rest of us. I thought about how miserable he must be, stuck in a wheelchair.

I watched him and noticed he seemed to be lonely. Instead of walking over to him and introducing myself, as a sensible person might do, I just kept my distance. Our little town had a few stores in an area usually referred to as "Downtown," and there was a small café where you could get a good meal. It's where everyone went if they didn't want to cook at home.

Late one afternoon I noticed the little boy in the wheelchair sitting at a table in the café next to his mother. Across the street was a novelty-type store; really more of a junk store. It was one of those places where you could find almost anything as long as it was something you didn't need. It was a perfect place for a kid because on nearly every shelf there was something that was entertaining, at least for a few minutes.

I was a frequent visitor in that junk store, but I seldom had any money to purchase anything. When I spotted the wheelchair kid in the café, I immediately thought about the store across the street. I knew there would be something there to make him happy, and that's what I wanted to do.

I scampered across the pavement toward the store, having a pretty good idea of what part of the area I would search. The thought of not having any money never occurred to me; I was too busy with my quest. As I neared the store, I slowed my run to a fast walking pace. I knew to look on the counter next to the front windows. That's where they kept the stuff that appealed to kids in hopes they would drag mom and dad inside to make a purchase.

Of all the toys and trinkets on the table, the one that caught my eye was a battery-powered dog. When the switch was on, the dog would turn its head, make a few weak barking noises and flip over like he was jumping. That was it. I knew the boy would enjoy this toy and it would be enough to keep him company.

My decision was made even easier when I looked underneath the counter and saw a stack of boxes filled with the flipping dog. I grabbed one, and I was so excited about getting it to the wheelchair kid that I gave no thought to taking it to the front counter and paying for it—I didn't have any money anyway. I just ran out the door and hurried across the street to the café to share my prize.

Entering the café, I was glad to see he and his mother were still at the same little table. I went up to him, handed him the box with the dog, and simply said, "Here, I want you to have this."

His eyes beamed and his mother smiled at me. I knew what Santa Claus must feel like when he hands out gifts to kids. His physical malady must have been confined to his legs because he had no trouble opening the box. He set the dog on the table next to his plate. I reached over and showed him how to turn on the switch. The puppy squeaked to life and then turned a perfect flip as he kept on barking. The boy laughed as his mother looked at me and said, "Thank you. That's so sweet."

I walked out the door feeling better than I ever felt before. In fact, I felt so good that I wanted to do it again. I hurried across the street, carefully avoiding the sparse traffic, back to the junk store. Once again, no one noticed as I entered, went directly to the front counter, picked up another box with a barking puppy, and shot out the front door. I was bursting with joy and anticipation as I crossed the street back to the café.

Without any hesitation, I went straight to the table where they were sitting and handed them the second prize puppy. I guess I was expecting the same reaction as before, but this time it was tempered a little bit, but I still enjoyed the experience. In fact, I enjoyed it so much that I did it two more times. Four boxes of dogs in all.

Obviously, the mother was not oblivious to what was happening. She watched me cross the street to the novelty store and saw what I was doing. Contacting the police, she reported me for stealing. They came and spoke with the store owner who had me arrested for stealing. Nine years old and now I was a criminal—officially.

Not only was it the first time I was ever arrested, but to be honest, the whole experience is also the last time I remember feeling good about anything. I genuinely felt good about what I had done for the boy in the wheelchair. Age nine proved to be quite a milestone in my life.

Needless to say, there was immense consternation at my house that night. It was quickly apparent to the authorities that sending me to my parents was not a good plan, so I was placed in juvenile detention for 30 days. It was evident to everyone that I was the youngest one there, so I had to fend for myself and not be bullied by the other kids.

I survived the month of detention and arrived home to the news that my stepfather had actually adopted me. To this day I'm not sure why. I have no idea what he wanted. I was nothing more than a punching bag to him, but he was the only father I had ever known, so I had no choice but accept it for what it was.

Leaving juvenile detention after 30 days was certainly not the end of anything for me. After getting released from the detention facility, I still remember the way people treated me differently. Some were quiet—too quiet. Others were outspoken about the fact that I was trouble. Then there were those who just avoided me and ordered their kids to stay away from me.

I remember Alex, a cute little blonde-haired girl about my age, nothing unusual about her, always nice enough to me. She would ride her bike up and down the road in front of our house. I remember she had things on her tires that made noise that sounded like shuffling cards. It bugged me, and I don't really know why. I think because I didn't even have a bike let alone noise makers.

I used to tell her to get off my road. She just kept riding by ignoring my nine-year-old taunts, although I had learned how to use some choice words in detention. Well, one day as she was riding by, I waited, holding a stick in my hand. When she rode by, I stuck that stick in her front wheel spokes. The plan was to make her stop, and I didn't realize it would flip the bike. However, it did. It was gruesome when she went into the sidewalk face first.

She was bleeding and crying loud, almost hollering. I noticed that she even lost a few teeth. I knew I was in big trouble, so rather than help her I began to beat her up even worse. That was my first act of truly unprovoked violence.

I ran to our house and up to my room, or the closet they called my bedroom. It was wide enough to fit a queen size mattress that touched the wall on both sides, and there was less than a foot between the bottom of the mattress and the door. The light was turned on by pulling a string from the ceiling, and there were no windows to allow any other light.

I waited for a long time, maybe as long as an hour, and it finally came—the dreaded knock on the front door. I could hear talking but couldn't understand what was being said. Then it came, "Erik, get your ass down here now."

When I descended the stairs, I saw my dad and the deputy sheriff. The look of fury in my dad's eyes was unmistakable. The sheriff asked me what had happened, so I recounted the story I had created in my mind. I told them we were playing "He Man" and the stick was my sword. I didn't mean to hurt her.

I thought he believed me because I didn't get arrested. Instead, he issued a ticket and said I would have to go to court. He thanked my dad and me on his way out the door. My dad walked him out as I sat at the kitchen table and waited. It only took a few minutes for him to walk back into the kitchen and I knew this was gonna' hurt.

Coming through the kitchen door, he grabbed a fly swatter and started toward me. I didn't move. I knew better. He began hitting me from the shoulders down. He beat on me for at least five minutes. With each swat, he said, "You little son-of-a-bitch, you like hitting girls."

To be honest, him saying that was a bit strange to me because he always hit my mom and she was a girl.

Broken

It seems that a life pattern had already been established. It went something like this - steal, lie, sell drugs, and get arrested. After a short time of incarceration, I would go home, get beat up by my father, and start the cycle once again. I made my way through a variety of group homes and lockups, neither one any better or worse than the other.

At the age of 12, I came home after a brief time in a group home, to discover that my mother and adoptive father had divorced. For some unknown reason, she insisted that he have visitation rights. I guess she thought it would be good to get me out of the house occasionally and give him the opportunity to continue the beatings.

One evening I came home late from a volleyball game at school. I was twenty-five minutes late because of a flat tire. The girl I was with actually went to my house to speak to my father and confirm that we indeed had a flat and that I had been most helpful. He said, "All right," but when she left, he said he was going to spank me. Defiantly, I said, "No!"

Without any hesitation, he hit me square in the face. I went down like I had been shot, blood gushing out of my mouth as if I was going to be lying dead in a pool of my own fluid in a matter of minutes. He had to transport me to the hospital where we discovered that the cartilage in the bottom of my mouth was broken. It couldn't be fixed, so they had to remove my lower teeth in the front of my mouth.

By this time, it was obvious to everyone that I could not survive the abuse of living with either of my parents. I don't know why they were not arrested and locked away from us kids. Perhaps it was because I was the only one of the bunch that was ever physically abused, so the logical conclusion was that I was just getting what I deserved. I really have no idea.

When I was 13, I finally got out of that hell hole and was sent to live with my grandmother and step-grandfather. However, it didn't take long before I realized I was just moving into another hell hole with a different kind of abuse. Things were different in many ways at my grandmother's house. She and my step-grandfather lived on three acres of wooded land. Their house was a 35-foot single-wide trailer, but she had built an addition onto the side, so it was more like a double-wide on the inside. The original was a typical shotgun style layout. When you walked in the front door, you were immediately in the living room. As you walked on into the house, you first passed through the kitchen and dining area before entering a hallway that led to a bedroom and a bathroom.

I stayed in the front bedroom with my grandparents occupying a bedroom that was constructed in the add-on section of the trailer. It was a little odd because they kept the original kitchen, but there was also a kitchen in the new structure.

After carrying my stuff inside and unpacking, they called me to the kitchen table to go over the rules of the house. It was simple—go to school, get good grades, and don't cause problems at school.

My grandmother was an average size woman. Her hair color was obviously artificial because there was never any gray. The clothes she wore were nearly always dirty, not from a lack of washing, but just because she worked so hard every day. Every day except one, that is, when she had her "go to town" day.

She refused to shop in the store where people in the community shopped. One day when she purchased her supplies, including several hundred dollars' worth of cat food, she was twenty-nine cents short of being able to cover the bill. The cashier joked that she would send a bill to my grandmother. Not having a sense of humor, my grandmother drove home, snatched up the necessary amount of coins and returned to the store. As she slammed the money on the counter, she vowed she would never come back to the store again. As far as I know, she kept that vow. So once a week they drove fifty-two miles to a neighboring town to load up on supplies.

My grandmother always had hundreds of cats around the outside of the house, many of them were sickly looking with matted eyes and ratty fur. Inside there were probably another fifteen house cats and a dog, an Australian Shepherd. That stupid dog was always eating tuna and those Fig Newton cookies, you know, the chewy, soft ones. He got so fat from his terrible diet that I had to haul him around in a wagon.

Imagine fifteen cats and an obese old dog in a small trailer house. The place smelled like a neglected kennel. The odor was even worse because my grandmother did all her cooking on a wood stove inside the house, so it always felt like it was 110 degrees. The cat hair and stench permeated the place, and even though I lived there, I never got used to it. She did work hard to keep it clean, I guess, up every morning at around three vacuuming the floor. My grandmother essentially took care of the place by herself since my grandfather was as lazy as their fat dog.

And I had one chore, milk the cow in the morning. The first morning at 5:30, there was my grandmother waking me up, time to milk the cow. I dressed and followed her to the barn. There was no such thing as an automatic milking machine; it was all done by hand. She grabbed the bag of balm which is a substance like Vaseline to keep the cow's teats from chaffing. Then she proceeded to show me how to milk a cow. Fifteen minutes later she had a bucket of milk.

Milking a cow is not difficult, but there are some important tricks to the trade. The main thing is to keep the animal from resisting. Watching my grandmother helped a lot, but it would have been nice to have a little more experience before she turned me loose on my own the next morning. My first day alone required a bit longer than fifteen minutes—it was more like two hours. I finally had a bucket of milk, along with everything else that stupid cow could kick into the bucket.

I've always been a quick learner, and that was true with the cow and me. I got good, and believe it or not, me and that stupid cow formed a friendship. It helped when I began taking sugar cubes to my room in order to coax the cow to my bedroom window. Soon, every morning at 5:30, that cow was standing at my window mooing like an alarm clock.

I loved farm life, but it was confusing. It was not all about caring for animals. My grandmother butchered chickens, ducks, rabbits, or anything else we could eat. I know you're thinking that's not weird, but she never explained any of it to me. Don't forget; I was still an impressionable young kid. I saw headless chickens running around spurting blood after she had cut off their heads. They flopped around on the ground for the longest time, and there was no explanation from her about what was happening.

One day I came home, and she said, "Let's walk."

As we strolled out to the field, the cow came up rubbing her nub horns on me like she always did. Grandma had something in her hand, but I didn't know what it was. It looked like some kind of caulking gun, but I never asked what we were doing.

As the cow was getting a good petting by my hand, Grandma took the instrument in her hand and put it up to the cow's head. There was a loud thump, and the cow fell straight to the ground, jerking around at my feet. I stood there in shock. I had no idea what had happened, and she offered no explanation. All she did was turn around and casually walk back to the house.

Something just struck me as I wrote those words. I always believed my grandmother was the one normal person in my life; my small island of sanity in an insane world. But as I ponder the description I just provided, it's obvious she really was not normal at all.

My Grandfather slept all the time, but grandmother was a light sleeper, and she always heard the noise I made, no matter how little, whenever I came in at night. I knew that as soon as I closed the door, I would hear her call out, "Erik, is that you?"

I always answered, "Yes Grandma, go back to sleep." She was then quiet for the night, and I would go to bed.

Grandma didn't like to be kept up late because she climbed out of bed very early every morning. There was a lot of work to be done, and I've never known anyone who worked harder than she did. From early morning until she came in to fix dinner, Grandma never stopped.

One evening I came home with a girl, Angie. We had been on a date, and we weren't finished so I decided we could go to my bedroom. I warned Angie to be quiet, and I tried my hardest to open the door without making a sound. I thought I had been successful until I heard the unmistakable question, "Erik, is that you?"

I don't know what I was thinking, but I made the decision to remain quiet, hoping she would just go back to sleep. I didn't say anything and gestured for my girl friend to stay silent. We started to tiptoe back to my room when all of a sudden, I heard a loud explosion and a bright flash filled the dark room.

I knew immediately what had happened. My grandmother always slept with a loaded shotgun next to her bed, just in case someone tried to break into the house at night. Well, it finally happened. The only problem—the burglar, was me.

Fortunately, one of the few things my grandmother didn't do well was aim a gun. Even though it was a shotgun at close range, she missed me completely. In the midst of all the screams and commotion, I was able to reassure her that it was me and that everything was fine.

Although my grandmother was vigilant and aware of any noise that might potentially be a burglar, she didn't seem to hear all the commotion that went on in her house. From the time I moved into their house until I was fifteen years old, my grandfather could be heard skulking around the house in the middle of the night.

I know that not because I was listening for someone who might want to rob our house, but because he always showed up in my bedroom. It didn't happen every night, but it did happen often enough that she should have heard him. I'm confident that she heard and knew what he was doing; she just didn't care.

My step-grandfather had a stocky build of probably about 200 pounds on his five-foot-ten-inch frame. He had the gray hair you would expect on a man who was sixty-five years old. He was always unshaven; even though he didn't have a thick enough beard to have hair on his face. I never knew why, but he was missing all but six teeth in his entire mouth. In addition to lacking teeth, he was also missing two toes on his left foot.

It seems like every time I saw him in the house; he was reading a Louis Lamour book. In addition to the odor from the house pets, you could always smell my grandfather because he covered his chest with *Ben Gay*. Obviously, he wore old people's clothes, his favorite being light blue polyester pants, and a white flower shirt. Whenever I saw that outfit, it made me think of a 1960's Go Go Dancer, or that maybe he stole the shower curtains to make his clothes.

It all came to a culmination when I came home late one evening after an especially trying day. I don't remember why, but it had already been a particularly difficult day. One of those days when I was at the end of my rope as they say. I told myself that if he comes into my room, I was going to put a stop to it.

I heard him open the door and enter my room just as he had done many times before. He never tried to be exceptionally quiet because there was no way I could ever sleep through the experience. Even without turning over to see him, I knew he was wearing his yellow pajama pants, the color of a street sign, with the gaping hole in the front for easy access.

The abuse I suffered at his hand was not the physical beating like I got from my parents. It was sexual in nature. It happened often enough that it almost seemed normal. In some ways, I was relieved that it was not nearly as bruising and painful as what I was more accustomed to experiencing.

Lying on the bed with my face toward the wall, I felt the covers lift off me and then he climbed into bed next to my back. He pressed his body up close to mine and reached around with his big right arm and grabbed me. It was not unlike what he had done numerous times before, but for some reason, I reacted with rage and fury. I decided it was time to put a stop to this. I said, "I don't want this tonight."

He didn't want to raise his voice so my grandmother could hear from the other side of the house, but he growled, "It doesn't matter what you want, as long as you live in my fucking house, you're going to do what I say!"

At first, I just tried to push him away, hoping he would stop with little resistance. But he continued and was demanding, so I said, "No!" But he kept at it.

I flipped over in the bed, jumped to my feet and began to pummel him with my fists. As you might imagine, I had a lot of experience fighting and punching, so I knew how to hurt someone. He fought to get up from the bed, and he tried to grab me to stop the punches. We wrestled around for a bit until I was finally able to shove him into the corner where he slammed up against the wall.

I can still remember the sounds of that fight—the reverberation when my fist struck his nose and blood started flowing. I knew his nose was broken.

He was obviously in agony as he curled up in the corner next to my closet. I don't know why his moaning didn't bring my grandmother, but she was nowhere to be seen. I distinctly remember the sound of my fists beating against his skin, and I stood there for a few seconds realizing he was unconscious. From the time he entered my room until he was unconscious in the corner was less than two minutes at the most.

I stood there thinking, "This fucker doesn't deserve anything."

My next move was to turn toward the door and dash to the kitchen. I knew exactly what I needed to do in order to stop this from ever happening again. In the kitchen, I went directly to the draw where grandmother kept her knives, yanked it open, and grabbed the first one that touched my hand. All I could think was that I had to stop people from treating me this way. When I returned to the bedroom, he was still curled up in the corner, in that state between consciousness and unconsciousness. In my mind, I was analyzing where is the best place to stab someone—do you stab them in the stomach, the chest, the heart, the head? In the leg? Am I just trying to hurt him?

I walked over next to him still not sure what to do. The first stab went to his neck. Even though I'm right-handed, I was holding the knife with my left. I have never been able to do anything with my left hand. Consequently, there was no force behind that first stab and no real puncture.

At that point, he seemed to realize what was about to happen, so he reached out for me. I was standing off to his left. With the knife in my right hand, my second stab went directly through his Adam's Apple. The craziest part to me was how fast blood accumulates. The blood splattered all over to the wall three or four feet away.

Once that stab occurred, I don't remember what happened very well. I just started stabbing him all over, twenty-nine times altogether I learned later. There were marks on the wall behind him where the knife went clear through his body.

In spite of being a light sleeper, my grandmother never woke up, so I went and got in the shower. While there, I heard her screaming, and it was an ominous moment. I was calm, not scared, kind'a not sure what had happened, but also thinking that he got what he deserved. I stayed in the shower and was still there when the sheriff came in. They never drew their guns. He instructed me to put on my clothes and come out. When I did, he asked me what had happened. I answered every question and told him everything. I showed no emotion because I didn't really care what had happened.

They called my mother, and when she came over, of course, she said there had never been any abuse. I was handcuffed and taken to jail. My life was about to take another turn, and once again, it was not in a good direction.

Fragmented

After I killed my grandfather, I was transported to Pendleton, Oregon, to the juvenile jail. At the time, I was obviously a minor, so my mother had control over all of my life. This included any legal rights. I could have fought to change that situation but to do so, I would have had to argue that I was mature enough to be considered an adult. That was a double-edged sword because if the courts agreed, I would have been charged as an adult and the sentence would be much harsher.

Against my wishes, she instructed my attorney to plead guilty. They took her plea on my behalf, and I was sentenced to juvenile detention until the age of twenty-one. Because of my age, this was the longest sentence they could impose.

Three things flooded my mind as I entered this place. You are instructed to always walk in front of the guards with your hands clasped behind your back, and every door has to be buzzed open. The second thing is the glass and lack of privacy. You can be in one room and actually see clear across the building to the housing area. The third thing is the noise. If you have ever walked into a dog kennel, then you know what I'm talking about. It's quiet in the office area, but once you open the door, there is a flood of noise.

There were kids and staff everywhere. Some were playing ping pong and others sitting at tables in groups or by themselves. It resembled any school across the country, except for the uniforms and type of kids. Everyone was wearing an ill-fitting jumpsuit.

My first time at this place was just thirty days when I stole the toy dogs for the boy in the wheelchair, but I knew this time I was going to be much longer.

The guard ushered me into a room that was labeled, "Intake," and ordered me to sit on a solid wooden bench. The guard's name was Aaron Wallace. I remember him because he had long hair and an attitude. He started peppering me with questions—"What's your height? Eye color? What's your mother's maiden name? Father's name?" and a bunch of other stuff like why I did what I did and what did I feel as I was doing it. I just tried to answer the questions, but he seemed mortified at my crime.

Once he finished with his questions, Wallace pointed me to the bathroom. I knew it was time for the fag guard to get his jollies. I swear, he only had that job so he could see young kids naked. I already hated him. He told me to strip everything off, even my underwear. He had me turn my socks inside out and shake my underwear.

Then I had to open my mouth as he peered inside. He also ran his fingers through my hair. Then he ordered me to lift my nut sack, turn around and spread my ass cheeks. I will say that this was one of the few rooms that you can't see into from the outer area. It was a sterile-looking room with nothing more than a stainless-steel bench, an open shower, and a mirror on the back wall.

He told me to take a shower and make sure I use the medicated soap. I was glad when he left the room. When I got into the shower, it felt private. When I pushed the water button, the spray was so fine that it made the water feel cold. I didn't care; the water felt good. I remember putting my head back and allowing the water run all over me, almost like it was washing away more than sweat and dirt.

I struggled with my thoughts during those few minutes. I just couldn't believe how I ended up in this mess. What am I going to do now? Where is my life headed?

While deep in my thoughts, I caught a slight movement in the corner of my eye and realized I was being watched through the mirror. I grabbed the towel and dried myself quickly. An orange jumpsuit was on the bench, but there was no underwear and a pair of socks with holes large enough to resemble Swiss cheese.

I put on the jumpsuit, and it was far too big for me—it had to be triple XL. I thought, "Do I look like a fucking triple XL."

When I was dressed, I pounded on the door and yelled for the guard. When he finally came in, I complained about the size of the jumpsuit. He told me to wear it for now, and he will bring another one to my cell.

We left the Intake and walked to my cell with my hands clasped behind my back. The walk took us through the housing unit. It was loud. Everyone thought he had to talk louder than the guy next to him. They were yelling about "fresh meat" and saying,

"He's mine, I'm gonna make you my bitch!" I also heard an abundance of racial slurs like "White boy" and "Cracker."

When we approached my cell, the guard yelled, "Rack 205" and it slid open.

I stepped into a small room with a concrete slab jutting from the wall with a mattress on top. There was a stainless-steel sink, and a toilet bolted to the wall. There was a window, perhaps three feet tall and six inches wide. It had been scratched up so badly you couldn't see anything, but at least I could see light and dark.

Alone in the cell, I finally had some privacy. No one was watching, and there were no handcuffs. The noise was still overpowering, but I could sit on the bed with my hands cupped around my ears and think about how to make sense of everything.

A couple of hours went by and my "bean chute" opened up. This is that covered opening in the door that is used for sliding in trays of food to the prisoner. The dinner was something that looked like meatloaf and tasted like a glob of hamburger overwhelmed by sweet ketchup on top. Also on the plate were runny mashed potatoes and green beans with a large chunk of fatty bacon in the center.

When I first arrived, they handed me a cup containing a stubby toothbrush, a tube of toothpaste, and a bar of soap. This is the only cup available for drinking, so when you hand it out the door, they fill it with a colored water solution referred to as Kool Aid. I didn't care. I ate every bite of that first meal.

The best word to describe the remainder of the night is long. All night, doors were buzzing open then slamming shut. It was as if those niggers didn't get enough talk time when out of their cell, they felt the need to yell at one another from across the Day Room.

Another obstacle to sleeping was the blanket. The wool was itchy, and there was not a sheet or pillow. The mattress was covered with plastic, and every move created a rustling sound that was amplified by the concrete walls. As you might expect, the guard never brought a better fitting jumpsuit, so I constantly felt like I was drowning in material.

Long before I was ready (I later discovered that it was 4 AM), the bench chute opened up, and a Styrofoam tray found its way inside my cell. The guard grumbled, "If you want this, you better get your ass up!"

Biscuits and gravy with rock-hard biscuits and gravy that must have been fifty-percent salt. It was all I could do to wash it down with the small carton of warm milk. But, once again, I ate every bite.

This was followed by a couple of hours of nothing more than pacing and thinking. I wanted a book to read; anything to get my mind somewhere else. Finally, I yelled, and a guard came to see about my problem. I told him I needed a book and he promised to see what he could find. For some reason, I knew what he really meant was to sit down and shut up.

There was a rattling in the intercom, and a man's voice instructed me to get dressed and line up outside my door with hands behind my back. I donned my oversized jumpsuit that I could barely keep on, as I stepped out and looked to the side, the guard yelled, "Eyes straight ahead!"

We stood there for a couple of minutes until everyone was in line. At that point, the guard shouted out, "Chow," and everyone turned and headed toward the Chow Hall.

The Chow Hall wasn't large, and it was filled with stainless-steel tables, and round chairs bolted to the floor. We all walked in single file toward a square hole in the wall. Someone on the other side shoved trays through one at a time. When it's your turn, you take a tray of food, and it then becomes one of the few times when you get to make a decision for yourself.

The decision is important because if you chose to sit at a table of niggers, the white boys are offended and the niggers aren't going to like you either. If you sit with a group of weak kids, then you spend the next week trying to prove you're not like them. There's also a table for the "Chimos" (child molesters), but I'd rather be dead than have one of them for a friend. Even sitting alone can be a problem because it's unlikely that everyone will leave you alone and let you eat in peace.

One of the characteristics of jail, any jail, is the monotony. Almost every day they served the same menu for lunch–two hot dogs, macaroni, cole slaw, and milk. Prison authorities viewed the meals as a means of providing nutrition. Prison inmates often had a different perspective about meals. It was used as a means of intimidation and proving dominance.

On my first day, luckily I didn't have to make that decision. Some half-breed nigger came up to me and declared that he was taking my hot dogs. I smiled at him and said, "If ya want it ya gotta take it."

He grabbed my hot dog, and I dropped the tray and started punching. A bunch of his buddies joined in, and fortunately, a couple of white boys took my back. It ended up with eight of us fighting for our place in my new little home. Instead of hot dogs that day, all of us got seven days in lockdown. I became quite familiar with that place during my stay in juvenile detention.

It was known by the name "23 and 1" because we spent twenty-three hours in our cell and one hour out to shower and make phone calls. Occasionally, if I called enough (thirty times in a row), my attorney would talk to me. She would always say nice things and tell me I was going to be convicted and assured me that she was working hard to understand why I did what I did. Although I knew she was lying, I liked hearing it anyway.

I've never been a physically imposing guy, so whenever I showed up at a new place a lot of people would take a shot at me. It was just to make sure I knew my place and that I was beneath them in the hierarchy. It never took long before testing started. The reason for the fight didn't matter. This kid chose hot dogs as the prize. This was certainly not because he was extra hungry, but he was communicating that he could do anything he wanted to me. He was going to make a public statement that he was stronger than me, so I would stay out of his way from then on. That's the way prison works. It's all about everybody finding their place in the pecking order.

Even though I was not a physically imposing figure, it didn't take long for people to learn that if they went after me, we were both going to get hurt. It seems that's almost as important as winning the fight.

Attending school in lockup was not a right. It was considered a privilege. It was a privilege for those who stayed out of trouble. I can count on my fingers the number of days I was allowed to attend classes at Pendleton. The students who did well in school received an award called, "Top Gun." They got to wear a fifty-cent hat with the words, "Top Gun" written with a Sharpie across the bill. Those hats were frequently flushed down toilets. My claim to fame was beating up all the "Top Gun" kids. That's how I was—a violent kid. That's essentially all I knew about life.

From the perspective of keeping the rules, I didn't do well. However, from an inmate's perspective, I did rather well. Already accustomed to fighting and beatings, I didn't mind a good fight. I got in a lot of them. For some reason, I hated black people and spent a lot of time fighting them, but I didn't hold back against anyone who tried to intimidate me. Not only could I take a beating, but I also knew how to hand one out as well.

After I had been at Pendleton for two or three months, my door racked open one morning. I don't know what time it was, but I do know it was still dark. The voice through the intercom told me to roll it up, which meant I was being moved. When I asked where I was going, the guard just repeated the command to roll it up. I thought, fuck you, I'm going back to sleep.

I continued to ignore the command until a guard walked in, grabbed the mattress from the far side, and with no delicacy at all, rolled me off the mattress. Of course, I came up ready to fight, but as I did, he tackled me on the bed, cuffed my hands behind my back, and took charge. He was amazingly quick for an old fat guard.

I was shoved out the door and through the Day Room toward Intake. During the whole ordeal, I yelled racial slurs to anyone who could hear. I heard the entire place rocking with people screaming, kicking doors, and guards hollering for everyone to be quiet. I must admit, it was awesome.

In the Intake Room, there were ten more people who were being transferred. They told each of us to stand up, grab a uniform, and go into the bathroom and change when our name was called. I was sitting peacefully waiting for them to call my name. After everyone except me was called, I asked for an explanation. The guard told me they were not uncuffing me so they would just wait and have my uniform returned later. I made it clear that I wasn't happy by yelling and jumping around the room like an idiot for a couple of minutes. Eventually, they forced me to kneel in the chair and then put shackles on my ankles.

All of us were loaded onto a bus with the doors and windows shut and locked. It took nearly three hours, but we arrived at our destination. It was not an intimidating place upon first glance. It appeared to be just like any hospital in the country. The gate swung open, and the bus pulled inside. Two guards were standing outside, and we were instructed to form a straight line and enter the building.

Once inside, the handcuffs and shackles were removed. They put us in a large room marked, "Receiving." Once we were all inside, the door was shut and locked. I remember how I couldn't hear anything from the outside and it was almost impossible to talk because of the echo in the room. After three hours of just sitting, it's not surprising that everyone was getting testy and grumbling at one another. I could feel the tension rising. Even though we had all come from the same place, I didn't know any of the other prisoners.

Finally, they began to call us out one at a time. It was probably close to twenty minutes between each person's name being called. As I stepped out, one of the guards pointed to a bathroom. My first thought was, "Oh goodie, another guy gets to get his jollies at my expense."

I swore to myself that I would crack him if he did, but then my more rational self prevailed, "Just get through this one more time."

Once again, the same thing—mouth, fingers through my hair, nut sack, turn around, feet spread apart, bend over, cough. I got in the shower, but this time the guard stayed in the room. I washed quickly, and he handed me a towel and a uniform; this one was brown and it fit, although I knew it wouldn't matter if it didn't.

Once we were out the door, the guard pointed to a chair and grumbled for me to sit there. The next thing was to shave my head. This was not a fine haircut like you would expect from a barber. They just dove in and started shaving. Whenever my skin was nicked, I would speak out, but the only reply was to shut up. The entire process was incredibly dehumanizing, especially when you remember that I was just fifteen years old at the time.

The next step was to take my fingerprints. The guy doing it kept jerking me around, apparently not caring one bit about me or how I felt. I was nearing the end of my rope, resisting the urge to crack him upside the head. Finally, as nicely as I knew how at the time, I told him to "Fucking quit jerking me around."

He looked me straight in the eye and tells me that I'm not the only killer in this place. He continued by saying I might have scared them everywhere else, but in here I wasn't shit.

When he finished, he assigned me to "5 Star" and told me not to forget my box on the way out. I jerked up a drab gray box without even looking inside. I started off in the direction he had pointed. There were signs along the way indicating "1 Star" and "2 Star" and on up to five. Once inside 5 Star, I stepped up to the desk that appeared to be some type of registration area. I could feel the other inmates sizing me up like inmates always do. That's the process of determining where everyone belongs.

I knew the routine, so I was always doing the same to them. It seemed that about half of them were black, perhaps a fourth were Hispanic, and most of the rest were white. The guard sitting at the desk took my name and number and assigned me to Bunk 22 and told me to sit at Table 3.

It only took a quick glance around the room to spot Table 3 because of the large white letters painted on the table. My first thought was, "Great! Three Coons."

When I saw who was sitting there, I told the guard, "I won't sit there."

"You don't get to make decisions here," he replied, "Sit down, now!"

Once more I said, "I can't sit there." I'm thinking, "Of course, this dumb shit is gonna show me who's the boss."

It didn't take a genius to realize that I was in a no-win situation. I picked up my box and started walking toward the table. I saw a big lip nigger and think, with one crack; he'll go down.

As I neared the table, one of the guys said, "You're not sittin' here."

I kept walking because I knew there were no other options. When I got close enough, I sat my box down and took the first punch at the big lip spade, and it landed square on the side of his face. He went straight down to the floor. However, before I could do anything else, more people than I could count jumped on me. Let me tell you; they whipped my white ass.

All I did was hit the ground and "turtle up." I covered my face as well as possible, and I remember thinking I was grateful everyone had to wear Crocs. After about five minutes of being pummeled and kicked, a couple of guards broke it up. They took me to the Infirmary where they determined my nose was broken, both my eyes were swollen shut, and I had a broken rib. It felt like I had spent the night being tossed around in a clothes dryer.

The next three days were spent in the Infirmary before they released me back to my Star. They did get the point and decided that I should sit in a group with three other white boys. Things were much calmer, and we spent most of our days playing cards or dominoes and bitching about everyone and everything, especially the guards and niggers.

Lockdown happened every night at nine. That meant we went to the dorm, and they locked a wire door behind us. The only guard around was sitting outside the door at a desk. The result was twenty-three young, violent boys left together in a confined space. We called the place "Gladiator School" because of the fights. It would take guards a good three to four minutes to get inside if needed, so you damn well better be able to fight. You really had to take care of yourself, or you wouldn't survive long.

Fighting for yourself was not the only necessity. We were also expected to back up others in our group whenever a fight broke out. When I first arrived at MacLaren, I was constantly in lockdown. It took some time, but eventually, I earned enough respect that people didn't mess with me so much.

With fewer fights, I began to settle in and stay out of trouble. I was even allowed to attend school classes. I have always had a desire to learn. I liked to study and read, and I've always had the ability to take stuff in, understand it, and remember it. Every teacher I had recognized that I was smart enough to learn.

Not only did I learn from classrooms and school books at MacLaren, I also discovered a great deal of bad stuff. It was here that I learned an enormous amount about drugs—not only using drugs but how the business works. One of my table mates even taught me how to make meth. Even though it was a juvenile facility, it was not a good place for kids. MacLaren is where I really honed my ability to be violent. It's also where I first became associated with White Supremacists and the Aryan Brotherhood. This would prove to be very helpful later in my life.

When I was approaching age 17, I was relocated once again. This time it was to a camp called Riverbend in LeGrande. It was what they described as a transitional facility, which means the purpose was to prepare us to get along in society after confinement.

They put about a dozen of us in a van. I remember the long gravel road, probably about two miles that led us deep into the woods. When it came into view, it looked like a lodge, a large log cabin. Inside it was just a great big dorm. We were each assigned a bunk and given sheets and blankets. I was more low key at Riverbend. I talked with a few people and read a ton of books. I was just waiting for my time to get out.

At Riverbend, it was possible to run away because the dorms were open to the outside. I did several times, but never went far away. They always found me and brought me back, and I would lose a few privileges. I think the reason I didn't really try to get away is because I didn't have any place to go.

During my seventeenth year of life, less than a year after arriving at Riverbend, I was released from juvenile detention. Since I had originally been sentenced until age twenty-one, I was required to report to a parole officer every week for the next few years.

However, I had no place to go. Not only was there was no place to go, but there was not anyone waiting for me. I was not on anyone's mind, except my own. They gave me a check for $225.00, but I couldn't cash it without ID. I decided to settle in Baker City, a small town located on Interstate 84 as you leave LeGrande and travel southeast toward Idaho.

I checked into a pay-by-the-week motel in Baker City, and most of what I ate was obtained by stealing from grocery stores. My entire wardrobe was stolen from a country and western store in town. It consisted of boots, Wranglers, brush popper shirts, belts—all cowboy stuff.

There wasn't much to do in Baker City, so I spent most of my time drinking, doing drugs, and stealing anything not bolted down. I was arrested over and over for little stuff—drug possession, theft, simple assaults, drunk in public. I drank A LOT. I could out drink anyone. The Safeway in town had a liquor store where it was easy to steal Jack Daniels, so I could pretty much drink all I wanted.

I was taken to the Baker County jail at least ten times, so all the police knew me and my habits and hangouts. It was apparent to everyone who knew anything about me that my destiny was back into prison. The only unknown factor was what crime was going to make it happen.

I seemed to have a knack for finding people who liked to do things I enjoyed. This was especially true when it came to drinking and partying. I remember the last party before I went to prison. It was around a bonfire probably about 20 miles outside of town. The girl we rode out with left early.

A buddy and I got drunker than shit. Since our ride had already left earlier, we started walking toward town. At first, it was all laughs, but it didn't take long before the fun wore off. My mouth was dry as hell; I could hardly swallow, my tongue felt like it weighed about twelve pounds. That was always a good sign the hangover is just around the corner. One of us spotted a half-eaten pack of life savers tossed aside along the road. We didn't care where they came from; we ate those candies like it was an eight-ounce glass of ice cold water.

That's when we spotted the white van in the yard near a house. We snuck over and looked inside. The keys were hanging from the ignition, so we jumped in and started it up to return to town. However, now that we had transportation, we decided to get a friend of mine in the town of Halfway. She was a cute brunette girl, always smiling, fun to be around. She was even fun to hang with even if she didn't put out. But of course, Angie would put out if she liked you, and I think she always liked me.

After we picked her up and headed back toward Baker City, we passed a horse trailer. I stomped the brakes, put it in reverse, and backed up next to the trailer. We rifled through it and found two saddles, some saddle blankets, couple of lassos, spurs, cattle prods, everything a cowboy needs. We loaded all of it in the van.

In my drunken state, I thought I had hit the mother lode. I can't imagine how I'll spend the money from selling all this equipment to someone. Drunk and driving a stolen van full of stolen stuff, the logical thing to do is spend Angie's money to get a motel room. I promised her that as soon as I sell the stuff I will give it back to her, even more. I asked my buddy where he wanted to go, and he said he wanted to stay with us. However, I wanted to be alone with Angie so I dropped him off with a friend of his and we got a room.

I had big plans for Angie. Most of the night was spent drinking beer and playing quarters. The night ended much differently than expected. I awoke an hour or two later, fully clothed with a hangover from hell. I needed a cigarette and a drink of water. It was around 10:45 and check out was at 11 am.

I woke Angie and told her we gotta get up and get out of here. She suggested we go back to her house and recover. We can stay there a few days and figure everything out. We both drank about five cups of water from those little plastic motel cups and headed toward the van.

During the night, the cops had spotted the stolen van. Since they were not sure who stole it, they staked it out overnight, waiting for the thief to come and drive it off. Sure enough, we obliged. As we came out of our room and approached the van, we were swarmed by police. I was thrown to the ground and cuffed rather quickly. Angie, not knowing the van was stolen, was crying and screaming at me. I just put my head down and let them lead me to the car.

The owner of the van had reported it stolen, but when she was notified about it being found, she declined to press charges. She was just happy to get her vehicle back in good condition and not wrecked all to hell. However, I was not so fortunate with the owner of the equipment we had taken from the horse trailer. He did press charges even going as far as to press the district attorney to pursue a prison sentence.

The judge set my bond at twenty-five thousand dollars which meant it would cost twenty-five hundred dollars to get out. That might not seem like much to some, but it damn sure is a lot when you don't have it. So, I just sat back awaiting all the judicial bullshit to run its course. The first offer I remember getting was ten to fifteen years in the penitentiary. I told my attorney, "Piss off. You better do better than that."

In jail, nobody trusts any of the other prisoners. There is no personal sharing beyond basic surface information. It was possible to know what kind of work a person did but not know anything about how they felt about anything. Giving away too much information is a problem because you have to go to court. If you tell your cellmate too much, it might come back to haunt you during the trial. Once you get to prison, you've already been convicted, so there's more freedom to talk.

There was an unusual situation at that jail. They didn't have any type of snack bar available to the prisoners. In order to provide snacks, they would give us quarters and take us to the nearby city library. In the lobby were some vending machines where we could get corn nuts and candy and stuff. I decided to hold on to my quarters and instead, I figured out how to shake the machine and get a few snacks to fall down to where I could reach them. Of course, I got caught. Another charge was added to my docket.

During my time in the Baker County Jail, I met a significant number of prisoners who came and went. One of them was Derrick, and he eventually came to be one of the most influential people in my life.

He was my Bunkie in jail, and we got to know each other fairly well, at least as well as one could under the circumstance. He frequently asked if I knew anyone he could write. I told him I would see if my sister would write him. After a couple of days, he started asking me regularly about writing her. Finally, I gave him her address but told him I didn't promise anything. I don't speak with her much since neither of us cared much for the other.

He wrote to her, and I was a little surprised when a couple weeks later a letter from her arrived. We didn't talk much about their letters—he didn't say and I didn't ask. But I can say she wrote him a lot—a letter almost daily. Derrick was convicted and sentenced to four to six years after I had been there about a month. When he left to start serving his sentence, I figured it would be the last time I would see him.

The District Attorney offered me a plea bargain of 18 to 36 months in the pen. My attorney assured me that I would be out in nine months. I took the deal, and after sentencing, they returned me to jail. I waited there for two weeks for transport to take me to the penitentiary.

Once again at two in the morning, I heard, "Daniels, roll your shit."

I jumped up ready to go. I hurriedly packed my legal papers, just the stuff I acquired in jail all fit in a manila envelope. I rolled up my mat, blankets, sheets, and picked everything up like a bear hug and hauled ass to the door. When they racked the door, and I stepped out, I saw another twenty-five inmates all standing there with their stuff. After going through much the same procedure as before with the strip search then handcuffs, shackles and belly chains, they put us on a bus. The ride was as uninteresting as one might expect; a lot of people doing a lot of thinking and not knowing what we were about to walk into.

As unintimidating as McLaren Juvenile facility was, the Oregon State Penitentiary was much the opposite. It was imposing in every aspect, from the gun towers to the rows and rows of fence wire. I heard the gasps as it became visible. Men in uniforms leading dogs and the complete eeriness of knowing you cannot leave until they let you out.

The gate slid open to allow the van to pull inside. A guard opened the van door and told us to get out and line up facing the wall. Once everyone was standing with their nose toward the wall, we heard our first, "I'm in charge you better listen to me, or I'll smash you" speech. These speeches would be plentiful over the next sixty days.

After he had thoroughly scared the shit out of most of us, he told us to turn around. We were then instructed to enter the door and follow directions. Once again, the same as every other place, the strip search, fingerprints, shave your head and asked a bunch of medical questions. We were then released into the Fish Tank which would be our new home for the next sixty days. There is constant testing, both mental and emotional, to determine if we are violent, a potential snitch, and all the other stuff they want to know.

Perhaps you've heard the often told tale that when you go to prison, go find the biggest black son-of-a-bitch and punch him smack in the face. Many times I had heard the story, but no one ever told me how it ends. So, let me tell you how it really works.

After giving us bedrolls, they told us to get into the Fish Tank, the facility for housing new inmates. I walked in, sat on my bunk, and promptly spotted the biggest black guy I could find. He was probably the biggest guy I'd ever seen. He was at least six feet five and easily weighed three hundred and twenty pounds. I knew he was the one.

I sucked in a big breath of air, walked to where he was until there was only three steps between us, drew my fist back with everything I had, and made a flying punch into his face. I know I connected because he winced, but he barely moved.

We both stood there looking at one another. He angrily looked at me and said, "The guards can't see in the shower. I'm gonna fuck you up!"

He turned and walked to the shower. I knew he was correct; the guards couldn't see in there. It was now time for another one of those life altering decisions. I could turn and run and pound on the front door and tell them I was scared for my life. They would then take me and put me in protective custody, which might work for a while. Or, I could walk into the shower and take the ass whooping that was coming.

Once again, I sucked in a deep breath and chose to walk into the shower. I decided to put up a fight that this fat guy would never forget. When I threw open the shower curtain to step inside, all I saw was the biggest fist I had ever seen coming straight at my face like a full eclipse. He struck me so fiercely that I was slammed against the wall and was out—totally unconscious. There was no showing this big black boy that I've got heart.

I don't remember being conscious again until in the Infirmary. My head was pounding, and my uniform was soaked with blood. It felt like my teeth had been jarred loose. They gave me a few Aspirin, and when they asked what had happened, I told them I fell down the stairs. I know they didn't believe me, but I also didn't care enough to argue.

On the walk back to my cell, I thought, "Damn, I fucked up. Everyone's gonna fuck with me now!"

When I got to my cell, I met my new bunkie whose name was Peaches. Yes, Peaches. I'm not kidding. Some little fag and I hated fags. He told me I could have the top bunk. I climbed on my bed without even making a sound, I crashed. Every part of my body ached.

After a couple of days just marking time, I heard a familiar voice. It was Derrick, my old cell mate from Baker. I got off the bunk and went over to the bean chute. I yelled for him to come over. As he got close, he saw my face, which still looked bad although it was beginning to heal. When he got to my door, he asked what happened. I told him not to worry because I got what I deserved. He told me to sit still, and he would try to get some cakes over to me. True to his word, the next day he came with a bag of Debbies.

I was eating well, being treated decently by the guards, and thinking that punching the big black guy must have worked out because no one was bothering me. Derrick brought food about once a week, and he would also bring some marijuana to smoke or a cup of hooch.

The Fish Tank had about fifty cells, twenty-five per floor. Each cell had two bunks, one on top of the other. When it was overcrowded, which it usually was, they would throw in a boat. This was a temporary bunk that simply rested on the floor. Every prisoner spent the first two months in this place.

The sixty days elapsed rather quickly and then we were assigned to our living units. Derrick had spoken to the Sarge and convinced him to let me bunk with him.

Derrick stands about six feet two inches, and I guess you could describe him as lean, weighing about a hundred and eighty pounds. He kept his black hair shiny and clean. He was always tidy in appearance. Derrick is not a particularly handsome man, with pock marks and a couple of scars on his face. It is evident from first glance that he is in shape with well-defined muscles. He looks as unapproachable in a t-shirt and jeans as he does in a two-thousand-dollar suit. Although he was about forty years old at the time, he wore his age extremely well.

Derrick was a high-ranking member of the Aryan Brotherhood. For him, being in that gang was not just a form of protection;

he really hated blacks and loved to tell people about how horrible they were. At first, he talked to me like he wanted me to join the gang, but after awhile, he changed his tune and began to tell me to stay away from it. I was being recruited by several gang members at the time, but he made them stop, and even sent an order that anyone messing with me on either side, either for recruitment or to hurt me, would be met with retaliation. In short, he sent out word to leave me alone. In order to earn your place in the Brotherhood, it required putting in some work, which could mean having to kill or at least seriously injure a nigger. This would mean my sentence of eighteen to thirty-six months could quickly become life.

Although we were issued uniforms, we were allowed to wear personal clothes if we bought them through prison commissary. I didn't have much money, so Derrick bought me loads of stuff. Let me clear this up right now—I wasn't his bitch.

The time went by easily considering I was in prison. I did get involved in a couple of brawls and spent time in segregation, but when I got out, I always went back to Derrick's cell. He had everything you could want in his cell—television, VCR, carpeting, and food. We never ate from the kitchen; we just ordered food from the commissary and cooked it right in our cell. He continued writing to my sister the whole time I was in prison with him.

Even though most prisoners think they are smart, they're really pretty dumb. They always get caught. As I listened to Derrick, I realized he was smart when it came to doing things, but not smart enough to keep from getting caught. We talked a lot about that, and I told him many times that if he were as smart as he thought he was he wouldn't keep getting caught. For example, I told him that it was foolish to drive around in a car registered to your own name. Whenever the cops ran the license plate, they would know you were driving. I suggested that he start a company and register his cars under the company name. That way, when they checked the registration, it would show up as being owned by a business, and they wouldn't give it a second thought.

I guess he was impressed with my reasoning and that's why he groomed me to help him when we got out. That's also why he didn't want me to become a confirmed gang member. Being as clean as snow from that shit was a valuable asset on the outside.

The days turn to months and the months to years fairly quickly. Remember, I was told I would probably be out in nine months. Well not quite. Even though I felt I was doing well, the prison officials didn't see it that way. From their viewpoint, I still fought, cussed at the guards, and refused to follow orders. A little at a time, I lost all my Good Time.

Here is how it works. On an eighteen to thirty-six-month sentence you are eligible for parole at nine months. Well, my parole was rejected. So, I would be eligible again at eighteen months. At my eighteen-month parole hearing, I was again rejected. Now at twenty-seven months, it would be considered a no brainer, but with the fights and the disciplinary problems, I lost all of my Good Time and not eligible for early release. I ended up doing almost all of my time—thirty-six months. I went in June 15, 1996, and was released June 11, 1999, four days shy of a full three years.

When I walked out of that place, Derrick had a thousand dollars put on my books so I would have a little starting money when I got out. They handed me a check for $1,175.00. I have no idea why they always give a check since it's hard to cash. So, with my check and a bus ticket back to Baker City they opened the gate and just like that I'm on the loose again. Although I was free from confinement, I was not free from the relationships and lessons that I picked up during my three years of incarceration.

Crippled

It didn't take long after I was released from prison to settle on a new occupation—I became a drunk. In fact, I became quite skilled at my work. I drank all the time, and I was worthless. Even when I crawled into bed at night, I needed alcohol so much that I filled one of those 32-ounce McDonalds cups about half way with alcohol, added maybe a cup of water, and then drank it throughout the night.

I was one of the guys you often see lurking in the shadows of a convenience store parking lot. I was either sitting on the ground or stumbling around the parking lot with a bottle of Jack Daniels in my hand, guzzling it down as quick as possible. At some point during the night, I would somehow make my way into the store and grab a pack of cigarettes before returning to my unfinished bottle outside. Eventually, when the bottle was nearly empty, I would puke all over myself and then pass out. Sometimes they would haul me to the drunk tank, but mostly I would just wake up a few hours later and wander off.

When I first arrived in town, I convinced a woman to rent me an apartment by assuring her I would pay her in two weeks. It's amazing how gullible people can be, especially when they want something from you, like rent money. I knew I could stay there and party until she threw me out. It's not that easy to evict a tenant. We had a great bash going one evening, and I was staggering around near an open window. I was so drunk that I actually fell through the window from this second story apartment. I can remember hearing the "whoomph" as I bounced off the side of the building and hit the ground.

I survived by stealing everything—alcohol, food, clothes. There was no way in hell I was going to get a job. In fact, I don't even think the concept of working for a living ever crossed my mind. With everything I had been through during the first two decades of my life, I developed an entitlement mentality. I felt the world had screwed me and I was owed everything. I was going to show everybody and do nothing other than drink. Believe me; my drinking was epic. With the amount of alcohol I consumed, I should have been dead.

One of the unfortunate consequences of prison is that it puts bad people together and they do little other than talk about how they do their trade. Just through talking, you connect. When you live with a guy for a year or more, you get close. Derrick and I were together for two years, and I could tell you every trick he had.

I was the type of person who only cared about one thing—me. I would do anything to make money for myself. Although he was a 40-year-old man, he was just like me in this respect. All either of us wanted was money. The money intrigued me. While together in prison, Derrick decided to mold me so he could later use me to accomplish his purposes. I was too stupid to realize that he wasn't smart enough to stay out of jail.

Derrick was released from prison about seven months after I got out. He and my sister had continued to correspond during his entire stay. Once he was released, he kept bugging her to get in contact with me because he wanted to help, and he wanted my help. Since no one in my family gave a crap about me, we had minimal contact with one another. After a few months, she finally told me how to contact Derrick, and I did.

We got together a few times, and it helped with my drinking. I toned it down quite a bit, and Derrick got me to thinking about doing other stuff. One of my problems was that I had few skills and I didn't know anybody who could help. About the only skill I had was how to make meth in the bathtub, which is what I was planning to do, and the only people I knew were still in prison.

Derrick always had money, just like he did in prison. I'm not sure why, but he was just that kind of person. He wasn't particularly smart, but he was smart enough at doing things that would generate money. His biggest problem is that he would do it until he got caught, which he always did because he never figured that part out. What he saw in me was the ability to do things in a different way to avoid capture.

Much of his success was because of his connections through the Ayrian Brotherhood. At that time there were two major forces in California operating in the same sphere—the Ayrian Brotherhood and Hell's Angels. Those two groups ran everything. Derrick held a high position in the local chapter of the Brotherhood which brought him into contact with people from around California and even far beyond.

Even though I like money, I never had any. Derrick, on the other hand, always had money. He had another skill that would prove to be valuable for both of us—he could fly planes. I have no idea how he learned to fly, and he never actually explained it all to me, I just knew that he could. Consequently, he knew how to use his flying skill to make us a shit load of money.

At that time, the big cash business was marijuana. It was highly illegal in those days, and the authorities took it very seriously. Derrick knew that to make real money in the drug business, we didn't want to be selling small amounts to kids on the street. We had to get into the distribution business. Through some of his contacts, he made arrangements to bring loads of marijuana across the border from Mexico.

It sounds kind of crazy to describe it now, but it was really an ingenious plan. Derrick and I traveled to the Texas border town of Laredo. On the first trip, I was somewhat confused. We always went to the bus station and purchased a ticket to some town in Mexico across the border. He told me that we were going to fly back, but I didn't understand why. As soon as we crossed the border, we got off the bus at the first stop even though it wasn't our ticketed destination. From there we took a cab to this shitty place called, "Boy's Town."

It's difficult to describe Boy's Town. It was established in the 1960's in Nuevo Laredo as a place where prostitution is legal. In fact, for lack of a better description, let me just say it was like a giant whorehouse. We drove up to the front gate of Boy's Town, and the cabbie dropped us off. Apparently, he was not allowed to go inside.

This place was enormous, the equivalent of several city blocks. It was all built around the whore houses, but there were also cantinas and other shops, like a complete village. The girls were everywhere, and they charged anywhere between two and a hundred dollars. I can tell you that phrase, "She's as ugly as a two-dollar whore" is true.

I remember, our first time there I got in a fight over twenty-five cent tacos. I ordered four from the street vendor, but he only gave me three. When I complained, his reply was to accuse me of stealing one. We groused about for a few minutes, but neither of us wanted to cause major problems over a quarter.

After about twenty to twenty-five minutes, Derrick came back and signaled for me to hurry and go with him. As I caught up with him, he said, "We have to go right now."

We exited through the front gate and walked four or five blocks to get a cab. If you've ever been to Mexico, you know that cab drivers are crazy. Derrick told him where to go, and he took off like an angry dog chasing a cat. He was speeding around corners, but the scary part is that he kept turning around and talking to us in the back seat while he drove. The whole trip was a little unnerving.

When we got to our destination, the cabbie stopped on the edge of a big field. The only thing in the field was a really old and rickety airplane. I have no idea, but it had to be at least from 1949. The age of the plane was compounded by the fact that Mexicans never take care of anything. My impression was that it was a piece of junk and this was a scrap yard. However, Derrick assured me it would work. He said we would never get high enough to worry about a major crash.

Not only was it old, but it was also small. There was an area in the front for the pilot and then a small, cramped space in the back. I had to crawl back there with four duffel bags of marijuana. The door itself was an adventure. To open it, you had to pop the latch, push it out a little way and then slid it back. It was almost too tight inside the cabin to reach over and get it open.

Derrick fired up the plane, and it sputtered quite a bit, but he finally got it running to where we could at least move. As we began to move, I could feel the nerves rumbling in my stomach. I was not convinced that this rusty piece of shit was ever going to lift off the ground, and if it did, I was even more afraid it that it would take off and then pummel us into the ground. Derrick looked around to make sure it was clear. All the time we were getting situated, Derrick was listening to traffic on his headphones. I have no idea what he was trying to hear, but I knew we had to wait for something to happen. It had something to do with other planes flying in the area. We would take off and fly extremely low. Our low altitude and the presence of the other planes somehow made it difficult for us to be spotted on radar. That's why we had to wait to take off at just the right time.

I was jammed into a minuscule space, surrounded by four heavy bags of drugs. The dust inside the plane, the smell of the marijuana, and the noise from the engine made the condition even more uncomfortable. Derrick was correct about our altitude. I doubt if we ever got above three hundred feet. To be honest, I'm not sure that plane could have gone much higher, even if we needed to.

Derrick instructed me that when we get to where we were going, I was supposed to open the door, drop the bags out quickly, and slam the door shut. Then we would head back up into the sky. After about twenty-five minutes in the plane, we flew over a canyon. Derrick said this is the place as he began to lower the aircraft and get as close to the ground as we could without actually landing. Just like I had been instructed, I opened the door and pushed the bags out onto the ground. From there we flew to a tiny airport somewhere in Texas. Derrick landed the plane, and we got out and left.

I was paid $15,000 for my part of the trip.

That was a lot of money for me. In a few short months, I had gone from passed out drunk in the convenience store parking lot to having a wad of money in my pocket. However, all it did was prove how horrible I am with spending money. It was only a few weeks before it was all gone.

It didn't matter. We kept doing this over and over again. We always picked up the drugs in Mexico but would drop them off in different locations. It might be somewhere in the California desert or maybe a desolate place in Arizona. Derrick drew locations out of his hat and then he would inform others where we were going about forty-five minutes before we departed. That kept us from developing a pattern so we couldn't be traced.

We started out with four duffle bags stuffed with marijuana, but I got to where I could squeeze eight good size bags into that tiny space. I also devised an ingenious way to rig the door handle so that all I had to do was pull a string and the door popped open. Even though we were delivering more drugs, I was still paid the same amount of money--$15,000 every run.

We did this for some time, and I was finally in a position to fund a better lifestyle. Although I never became a financial wizard, I did learn to handle my money better. I rented an apartment that was completely furnished for $3,000 a month. I paid cash for cars and pickups. It wasn't like I was rich or anything, but for a twenty-two-year old, I was doing very well. I was able to buy almost anything I wanted.

When business is going well, it only makes sense to expand. Derrick decided he wanted to start doing stuff much further away in South America—Columbia to be precise. For decades, Columbia has been notorious as a drug provider for the United States. When we started going there, the money was much better. The downside is that the people we did business with were scarier. These were individuals who were extremely high up in the drug business, which gave them a lot of power. The process was virtually the same. Derrick and I would make our way to Columbia over land, pick up a plane, load it with drugs, and fly it back to a secluded spot and drop them in a drop zone.

While we were in Columbia, I was not allowed to do anything other than hang out in the plane. I didn't know anyone, and I'm not sure I wanted to know them. They were forbidding people who didn't like outsiders. As long as I was with Derrick, there was no problem. However, he would occasionally go to a party or something, and I always stayed on the plane. When it was time to go, men would stack the bags of drugs next to the wheels on the plane, and I picked them up and loaded them inside.

There was a time when I had an issue, and my only option was to get out of the plane. I looked at the buildings nearby, and it was a pitiful sight. It was like a bunch of huge cardboard boxes stacked like children's blocks on top of one another. It was unbelievable the kind of structures they built and used. They all knew who I was and that I was with Derrick, so no one said anything as I entered the building. Although the place looked like shit from the outside, once inside I confronted an amazing sight. There was money everywhere. Stacks and stacks of money all over the place. It had to have been millions of dollars. They had so much money they hired people actually to haul it from place to place.

Once or twice during the Columbia trips, we had fuel issues with the plane. We would be short and have to land for refueling before crossing the border. That always created a complication since it involved more people and movements. We always refueled in Mazatlan in Mexico, an area that was trying to keep the Cartels out. We were told not to worry about the Cartel stuff, just refuel the plane and move on. I was never high enough in the organization to understand exactly what was going on. I tried to do my part and keep quiet.

From Mazatlan, we flew north to a place just out of San Diego. Somewhere out in the southern California desert, there was a single airstrip. We would get low enough almost to touch the ground and I would drop the drugs out the door. We never landed or stopped the plane. From that point, we flew off to somewhere else where we would land the plane and be on our merry way.

At first, I returned to Baker, but just a few times. I didn't want to go back there because there was nothing for me but bad experiences and influences. I eventually moved to Boise, Idaho. I met a girl there who I really liked, and I stayed with her often. Even though I was doing better, I will still not a model citizen. I was arrested a couple of times in Boise, but not for anything serious.

However, our work never changed. We always picked up drugs in either Mexico or Columbia and then flew back to Texas or California. For some reason, I never stayed in either of those states.

We ran these routes for more than two years, taking a trip nearly every week. We hauled a ton of drugs across the border. I eventually quit drinking. Whenever I worked, it was always with Derrick. He always had schemes working with other people, but I never messed with anyone else. Derrick was my guy, and I trusted him completely. He was like a father figure to me.

During one of those times in between trips, I was in our apartment in Boise by myself. Even though our apartment was normally a crowded place, it was nice to have a few moments to myself. Early in the afternoon while I was stretched out on the sofa, the doorbell rang. Most of the people I knew never rang the bell; they would just walk in and make themselves at home. Assuming it must be a stranger, I went to the door. Once I pulled it open, I met a man who was about to send my life off in another direction once again.

Mangled

The apartment I was living in was just outside the city of Boise, Idaho. It's not like I had moved across country to get away from my past. Boise is just across the border from Oregon and is just a short drive from Baker City. I guess you could say it was the typical story of the country boy moving to the city. In hindsight, I probably should have moved much further away because my past was going to catch up with me.

The apartment wasn't part of a large complex like you often think of when you picture city apartments. Instead, it was a small collection of just three apartments connected by a hallway. The structure of the building was like a triangle, and you could access all three of the units from one corridor.

My place had a kitchen and living area on the first floor. It was spacious with a modern feel to the design and style. Off to the side was a staircase that led upstairs. At the top of the stairs, to the immediate right was a bathroom and to the left were two bedrooms. Compared to the rat traps and prison cells I had called home throughout my life, this place was high living.

There were also a couple of unusual rooms inside the apartment, the kind of rooms you don't typically find in most places. Solar energy was coming on the scene and high-altitude locations like Boise were great testing sites. The owner was attempting to operate everything in the apartments from that source of energy. One of the rooms was filled with batteries and other solar equipment.

The other unique room was downstairs, and it was more like a storeroom, or perhaps more accurately a junk room. What made it unique was the door, which was only about half the height of a standard door. If you bent way over to step through the door, once you crossed the threshold you could stand up straight. As you can imagine, we threw stuff in there just to keep it out of the way.

We even had a soda machine in our living room because Derrick knew a guy who worked down the road at a distribution center. It was kind of weird. When you wanted a cold beer or soda, you didn't open the refrigerator in the kitchen. Instead, we just hit a button on the machine in the living room.

Derrick was at the apartment often, and it seems like there were always tons of people. Dealing in drugs as heavily as we were meant that certain kinds of people would always find you. However, I never really got into selling drugs much. There just wasn't enough money in dealing to individuals. It was just easier to give it away to a few close friends.

We threw huge parties constantly. And there was always money. One of the most difficult things I had to do was spend money without letting others know how much I had. Once people realize you have money, they not only want some of it, but also, they want to know where it came from. If you're not careful, word gets to the authorities, and then you have a lot of explaining to do. It's best just to keep quiet.

That was hard for me because I still enjoyed spending money. I paid cash for a new 2001 Dodge pickup with jacked up axles and big tires. It was the typical hick truck. I also purchased a motorcycle and most anything else I wanted. I loved to spend money. Money was so easy to come by that there was no incentive to do anything else. It was the feeling that there was an endless supply.

I spent more than two years in the drug business, but even the most exciting of occupations can be tedious. Traveling south of the border and then flying back to the states, although it had some harrowing moments, was beginning to wear on me. I was at the point where I felt stuck, but I had no idea how to get out. The drug business is not just something you walk away from like a job at a fast food joint. Leaving creates all kinds of suspicions and people in that type of work aren't comfortable having co-workers leave the fold. I was aware that if I ever did leave the business I would disappear, either of my own volition or at the orders of someone else.

Although Derrick lived in other places, my apartment outside of Boise was the central hub of our drug business. That made it even harder to walk away. Although I wasn't the main man, I was directly in the center of every aspect of the business. We always left on our excursions from the apartment and returned once completed to the apartment.

I've known enough bad guys in my life to know that those who are caught are almost always unaware they are on the verge of being arrested. There's a feeling of invincibility when you get away with something for a long time. You learn how to be careful and you meticulously follow a routine that promises the most safety. However, there is a reason prisons are so overcrowded. Even the smartest are often not smart enough.

I had no idea at that time that our activities were being investigated by law enforcement authorities. Everything we did was spontaneous with hardly any planning. Usually, Derrick would simply say, "Come on, we're going," and next thing you know we were south of the border. Occasionally I would wire money to friends, sometimes as much as $15,000 or $20,000. I didn't think much about it, but those wire transfers put us on the radar with investigators. Like every criminal who gets caught, we didn't think of everything. There are just too many little details that get overlooked.

The day I heard the unexpected knock on the apartment door I was alone. Music was blaring through the stereo speakers and I was dozing in and out on the sofa. When I answered the door, I was confronted by an ordinary looking guy wearing jeans and a t-shirt. He was unfamiliar so I first assumed he had the wrong apartment or maybe he was selling something. There was certainly no reason to be alarmed.

I asked, "What do you want?" as if to communicate that he was bothering me.

He called me by name and said, "I need to talk to you."

Obviously I didn't recognize this guy, and while I was striving to figure out how he knew my name he introduced himself. He told me that he was with the DEA and asked if we could talk. When I heard "DEA," he had my attention.

I replied to his question with a firm, "No." There was no way I was going to get into a conversation with a narc. I knew they could be tricky, twisting my words to say whatever they wanted to hear. Even though I made a move to close the door, it was apparent he was not going anywhere.

Undeterred by my unwillingness to talk, he proceeded to say, "Here's what's going to happen..."

He laid everything out on the table and explained precisely what they knew and how they knew it. I must admit he was right on with most of his facts about our operation. He knew about Derrick and me flying drugs across the border and that we had been to both Mexico and Columbia. He also knew how we dropped them off without landing. He even identified dates of our travel that were accurate. About the only thing he didn't know was Derrick's connections across the border.

The DEA Agent explained what he knew about our travels, and he even had photos of me driving a truck in Mexico. It was obvious they had more than enough evidence to convict all of us, but they wanted even more from me. Apparently, they knew I wasn't the main man in the operation. It was really Derrick they were after. He never said why I was chosen to be the rat, but they had good reasons.

I don't remember being scared. I had already been through a lot in my life, and the thought of returning to prison, although not something I wanted, was not frightening. I was just ready to be done with the whole drug thing. I was restless, and it was time for a change. Obviously, it was time for a change in several ways.

I should have been frightened; not for what the DEA could do to me, but what giving in so easily would mean for the rest of my life. The stories you have no doubt heard about rats being the most disliked among criminals is certainly true.

He advised that I would be allowed to walk away scot free, no jail time. All they wanted from me was information and corroboration of their evidence. I quickly agreed to help. It's not like I needed time to make a decision. It was obvious they already knew what we were doing, and I was ready to do something different anyway, so from my perspective, it was a no brainer. I could either help them or be carted off to prison that afternoon. In hindsight, perhaps if I would have taken a little more time to think about things I could have made a better deal for myself.

I don't recall every being offered anything like witness relocation or protection. Honestly, I never thought about it. It didn't dawn on me that I might need some help once it was finished. Obviously, hindsight is always too late. I should have hit the road and disappeared that afternoon. It was evident the DEA was not that interested in me; they were after bigger fish. I might have been able to grab up the cash lying around the apartment and hit the road. My life might have taken a dramatic turn for the better at that point. It certainly couldn't have been any worse than where I was headed.

Before the agent left, he handed me a business card for a tree trimming service. On the back were a bunch of numbers and scribbles, designed to make the card look authentic. If someone were to see the card, they would not think anything about it.

After he left, three or four days elapsed and I didn't hear anything. I felt a little nervous, not sure exactly what to expect or when things would happen. I tried hard not to do anything that I wouldn't normally do. I gave it my best shot to keep an even keel, not act suspicious in any way, and hopefully, none of my friends would suspect anything.

It never occurred to me that my apartment could have been bugged. It was however obvious that they were keeping an eye on the place because when I was contacted the second time, I was home alone once again. This time the agent told me that I was going to wear a wire. It wasn't the kind of wire that you see in the movies where they make you take off your shirt, tape a wire to your skin, and hide a recorder somewhere on your clothes. Instead, he handed me a pack of gum—Starburst to be precise. I chew gum constantly, so there would be nothing unusual about me having a pack of gum with me all the time. He told me to carry it in my pocket and they would be able to hear everything.

During the next two weeks, we made a couple of drug runs, and they were able to record everything. One of those trips was to Columbia, and after we returned, they spoke with me several times, and I handed them the recordings and gave them all the information I knew. They contained several incriminating conversations with Derrick and others. I tried to pay close attention to the things I said during the recordings so they wouldn't be taken the wrong way.

I had no idea what the DEA was planning. They took the information I provided without telling me any details of what would happen next. But when they decided to act they came in a hurry.

Several of us were sitting around the apartment, just doing what we always did in between jobs, not much. I was slouched over in the easy chair, a not-so-cold bottle of beer in my left-hand dangling over the side of the chair. The TV was on a football game that we were half-heartedly watching, arguing about, and betting on. I've never been a huge football fan, you know, one of those guys who faithfully follows one team. I enjoy watching the game, but I seldom give a shit about who wins. Two guys were sitting on the floor. One of them was clutching a beer and I vaguely remember the other guy, kind of a newbie to our group, was emerging from a drug stupor.

Derrick was lying flat out on the couch. He had kicked off his boots and his feet were propped up on one end of the couch and his head was resting on one of those decorative cushions on the other end. Like usual, he was the center of everything. It didn't matter if it was a drug deal, a night out on the town, or sitting around watching football; everything revolved around Derrick. There was never any doubt as to who was in charge at all times.

I never crossed him once. Oh, we would argue occasionally about simple stuff or ideas, but when it came down to it, we always did what Derrick wanted to do. And I'm not complaining about that. As I've already said, Derrick was my mentor; the closest thing to a father figure I have ever had. I'm not sure if it's true on this particular afternoon, but it probably was—we were watching that specific game because Derrick said to. He liked to gamble a little on the side so it's likely he had a few dollars riding on the score. The quiet instantly disappeared when suddenly, DEA agents burst through the front door and scared the hell out of everyone.

The door crashed open like there had been an explosion in the hallway. Agents with guns drawn and pointing directly into the room started screaming and barking out commands. They were all dressed in black, covered with body armor and heavy boots, the kind you see soldiers wearing in combat. It was nothing short of a military invasion and I was on the wrong side.

"Get on the ground, now! Get your fuckin' ass down, on the floor now. Hands behind your back; get down!"

I was completely unaware that anything like this was going to happen that day, or any day for that matter. I'm not sure what I expected, but I didn't anticipate being on the wrong end of a raid and having guns stuck in my face. I guess I thought I would get a phone call some day from my DEA friend to tell me that Derrick had been arrested and I was free to go.

The agent I had been working with was in the group that smashed through the door. It was somewhat of a relief to see him. I knew we had a deal, so I wouldn't have to try and explain to anyone else why I was not going to be in trouble.

You don't need to tell me I'm not often the smartest guy in the room, but I've got to confess, on that day I was a total idiot. Not knowing what I was supposed to do, I just stood around like I wasn't worried, almost like an innocent bystander. If anyone had been paying attention they would have thought I was someone who had just stumbled into the wrong place at the wrong time. Everyone else was sprawled out, face planted on the floor fighting through the surprise and confusion. I stood over to the side like a rubber necker passing an automobile accident. They tried hard to make it appear like I was being arrested just like everyone else. They forced me to the floor and handcuffed my hands behind my back. They even roughed me up a bit.

To show you how naïve I was about what was happening, my primary thought was why are they treating me like everyone else. They told me there would not be any charges and I wouldn't have to go to jail. Fortunately, I didn't blurt out anything to that effect. I wasn't quite that stupid.

Once everyone was under control, they stood us up on our feet. Although it seemed much longer, the whole process didn't take more than two or three minutes. Agents quickly scoured every room to make sure everyone in the apartment was secured. I was beginning to gather my senses and get some stable bearings to realize it was crucial that none of my friends saw me receiving special treatment. Once we stood up, I tried desperately to appear as surprised as everyone else. I hurled insults at them, and even swung my leg as if to kick one of the them standing next to me.

At this point, we were marched out the door and shoved into waiting vehicles. Apparently, there were more people in the apartment than anticipated because there was not enough transportation for all of us. There were the four of us I described in the front room watching TV, I think two more were in the kitchen and one guy had just gone to the bathroom. Along with another guy, I was put in the back seat of a two-door car with bucket seats. When they left us alone in the car, we moved our hands from behind to in front by simply pulling our arms out over our legs. It's not hard if you have been in handcuffs as much as I have.

As I looked around the car trying to act like I was as surprised as anyone at what happened, I noticed the keys were in the ignition. Although we were still handcuffed, with them in front, it would have been incredibly easy to jump into the driver's seat, start it up, and drive off. I'm pretty sure we wouldn't have gotten very far, so we didn't even try.

Once everyone was situated in a vehicle, it was like a caravan to jail. It was quite a scene when we arrived at the courthouse. They herded us inside like a freshly rounded up herd of cattle. Each of us was put in a chair and ordered to stay put until our name was called. Although I went through the entire process, unlike everyone else, I wasn't actually booked into the system. I was released according to the agreement we had made several weeks ago, so I wasn't facing any charges. They were careful to keep all of us separate, and they waited until everyone was in their cells before releasing me.

I walked out of the jail that night a free man. However, once again I was without any plans for the future or direction for my life. The man who had been my mentor, perhaps the one person who had done the most for me in my entire life, was in jail. I was sure he didn't want to talk to me, and he would not be in any kind of position to help me with anything for a long time, if ever again.

I drove back to my apartment and parked outside for a few minutes before going in. I wasn't sure what to expect. While I was waiting to enter, I checked phone messages. There were close to a dozen on the answering machine. Word had spread quickly about the raid and I was sure everyone was calling to talk about what had happened. However, I only listened to a couple of the messages before it was clear that everyone knew what I had done. I was the snitch. I don't know how they figured it out so quickly, but it was no longer a secret. The messages were mostly angry death threats, so I knew it was time to vanish. My friends, the ones I had turned against, were correctly blaming me for what had happened.

There was no way they would ever give me a chance to explain that I had no choice. I tried to picture myself sitting across the glass partition in the jail visitor's room with Derrick perched on the other side. Just imagining his perfectly placed hair serving as an accent for the icy stare that often showed on his face when he was angry caused me to shiver. He would be sure to let me see his muscular frame as I tried to convince him there was nothing else I could have done. That wasn't going to happen.

I also knew that Derrick had enough connections that there was no need to wait for him to get out of jail before I needed to hide. The numerous messages on my phone were ample evidence that Derrick had already spread the word and I was a target for multiple people.

I knew I had to get into the apartment quickly, grab what I could find, and get out of town. If you've ever been to a place where police have conducted a search, you know what I mean when I say it was evident the entire apartment had been searched. The place looked like some kind of natural disaster had occurred. Nearly everything of any value was gone. They removed cushions from the sofa and even tore out the vent covers on the floor. The place looked ready for disaster relief efforts.

I looked around for anything of value, and one of the first places I looked was the room with the tiny door. The door was still closed and partially hidden by stuff scattered from other parts of the room. We used it for storage, and for some reason, the police missed it entirely in their search. As soon as I ducked down and entered the room, I discovered a small case, like a brief case carried by a business executive, and it was filled with money—nearly $175,000.

Further out of Boise I knew of a place where a guy was building a new house on some wooded land. Far behind his construction site, there was a small rustic cabin that no one ever used. I drove out that direction, carefully watching to make sure I was not being followed. Once I felt like I was alone, I entered the lonesome cabin. My plan was not to stay there, but to use it as a place to keep the money. It didn't seem to be wise to be carrying around that much cash. I opened the case and put some of the money in my pocket, leaving the bulk of the cash in the briefcase. Locating a small closet in the cabin, I poked it in a back corner, knowing it would be there until I could return safely. Then I ran.

I ran all over Washington, Oregon, and California. I went everywhere without any kind of direction or plan. The entire time I was as restless as a sick person waiting for bad news from the doctor. I still had my phone and was receiving frequent death threats. I finally had to obtain a new phone to get some peace.

The DEA, with all the information and evidence obtained in the raid, were not as desperate for my help any longer. This also meant they were not so eager to help me. In fact, I heard little from them until the trial was approaching.

Prior to the trial starting, I was contacted and asked to come to the prosecutor's office. Once I arrived, I spent an enormous amount of time sitting in a room being grilled about my testimony. The prosecutor drilled me over and over about what I was going to say and how I was going to respond to questions from the defense. They never asked me to change my testimony, but they certainly didn't want any surprises during the trial. I was as ready as possible when the trial began.

I was ready for everything except for having to face my former collegues. I knew they were angry—they had every right to be. It wasn't the fact that they were no longer friends that bothered me, I didn't really like any of them anyway. The real problem was that I was sure they would kill me if the opportunity arose. I had seen Derrick give order for such things before. Remember, he belonged to a notorious gang, one that had no problem with solving problems with violence. Although, through my prison stays I had learned how to fight and how to survive, it was different outside the bars. Opportunities for attack were endless and it was extremely stressful living in constant awareness of everyone around me.

The actual trial lasted six or seven days. Since witnesses were not allowed inside to hear the testimony of others, I sat outside the courtroom. Three police officers were assigned the task of staying with me for my safety and to make sure no one tampered with me. The most awkward part is that member's of Derrick's family and some of his friends were also outside the courtroom. You know what they say, "If looks could kill..."

On the day of my testimony, they escorted me into the courtroom at close to 11:00 in the morning. Putting my hand on the

Bible, I took the usual oath required of all trial witnesses. I looked over at Derrick and my hand quivered a little when it rested on the Bible. The whole experience was stressful, not just because of the importance of the trial, but because it was a public accusation against those who had been my friends. It was easier when I averted my eyes from the four defendants; especially Derrick.

They had all decided to stick together and use the same attorney. That meant they were unable to point the finger at each other, so I was the only one to blame. The prosecutor talked me through my testimony, and the defense attorney asked what I had been promised for turning on his clients. The defense strategy was to make it look like I was in charge of the whole operation and had turned in the others so I could get a free pass. I was testifying in order to secure a get out of jail free card, but there is no way anyone would have believed I was the leader. It was apparent just by watching him sit in the courtroom that Derrick was the boss. There was just something about him that gave off an aura of authority. Perhaps it was the perfectly turned-out hair or the brawny body. Or, it was probably the way everyone else acted around him. It was obvious to anyone paying attention that Derrick was a man to be feared.

The whole time I was on the witness stand, when I looked out over the courtroom, it looked like a room of high school girls with the amount of whispering going on, even a few of them mouthing threats to me.

The prosecutor walked me through testimony just like we had rehearsed numerous times, and the defense attorney peppered me with questions, but nothing I was unprepared to answer. My testimony was crisp and on point, unlike how I was feeling inside because of what I was doing.

In the end, all the defendants were found guilty and sentenced to at least five years in prison. Derrick, since he was leader of the operation was given a sentence of seventeen years in federal lockup. By that time, he didn't have anything left. The authorities had taken everything from him.

Although the trial was over, I knew the ordeal for me was not nearly finished. There was no way I could remain in the vicinity. In fact, with the reach of the Aryan Brotherhood, I couldn't imagine any place where I would be safe. I was out of the drug business and now I was in the survival business.

Damaged

Living inconspicuously is not easy for someone like me. I like to have stuff, to buy things, to enjoy life. However, at this point, I had no choice. People were looking for me, and I'm sure they would have killed me if given the opportunity.

There are hundreds of small towns in the northwest where a person can hide. Places that are far away from the usual traffic of tourists. Many of these places are surrounded by trees and sparsely populated by people like me—folks who want to get away from something and be alone.

My biggest problem was that I didn't like being alone. I like to party. And don't forget, I do like to drink. For about eight months after testifying at the trial and vanishing in the night, I bounced around a couple of these unremarkable places, making a few friends and trying not to stir up too much trouble. Finally, I settled in one of those places—Long Creek, Oregon.

I still had no marketable skills, so I had to rely on the one thing I did well—stealing. I became quite adept at taking other people's stuff and turning it into money to finance my life. There were a few skirmishes with local police, but nothing that would land me in serious lockup or long-term difficulty. I was that guy that no one really knew what I did, but I could always be counted on to show up at a party, bring some booze, and help everyone else have a good time. No one knew of my past.

If I had a weakness other than drinking it was girls. I met Jesse at a party and was attracted to her immediately. She had that one quality that always captures a man's attention—big boobs. I mean massive. She wasn't especially good-looking even though you could tell she worked at it. It was obvious that she spent time in front of a mirror before leaving the house. Her strawberry blond hair framed a non-descript face. To be honest, from a man's perspective, the time she spent with the mirror time was well spent.

Jesse wasn't fat by any measure, but a little heavy would certainly be an accurate estimation, weighing about a hundred and thirty-five pounds. Not only was she large upstairs, but her thighs were a comparable match. I only saw Jesse a couple of times, and she always wore nice, tight jeans and an exceptionally tight top. She knew how to accent her assets. She possessed that one quality that I think is most important in a girl. She is what I call "doable." Not only that, but she was also willing.

Jesse wasn't the town slut or anything like that, but if you hit it off with her at a party, it was likely that you wouldn't be going home alone. I first met Jesse at a party and, yes, we did hit it off.

We got along well. It wasn't a serious relationship or anything. We both liked to party, drink, and have sex. That was about as far as it went. In between, we talked some. She talked a little about her family, but I didn't pay much attention. I think she lived with some friends and waited tables at a local café. She was just nineteen-years-old, so she was still taking time to enjoy her youth.

There was an occasion when I opened up and shared some of my past. I didn't tell her everything, but I did speak of my time running drugs across the border. I thought it made me sound cool and she would be impressed. She was. She kept pushing for more information, and I eventually told her about Derrick and how his friends wanted to kill me. At the time, I didn't give it much thought, but it turned out to be a huge mistake.

The first time I realized my big mouth might be a problem was when Jesse came by the apartment where I was staying with some friends. She seemed a little desperate and said she needed some money—not much, just fifty dollars. Back in my money days, I would have just handed her a hundred-dollar bill without a second thought. Money was not as accessible now, so I was hesitant. Perhaps I was a little too evasive because she suggested she might tell my "little secret" if I didn't help.

For a brief moment, I sensed a rush of blood to my face, and I was flush with anger. How could she threaten something that could get me killed? The anger must have appeared as bright red on my face because Jesse immediately stepped back and blurted out, "Just kidding, I would never do that!"

I took a deep breath, one large enough to swallow my anger and slow enough to think what to do. I didn't know her well, but I had no reason to believe she would ever want to cause me harm. She just needed some money. I firmly grabbed both of her arms and made her look right into my face as I said, "You better forget that shit if you know what's good for you!"

I didn't mean anything by it. I was just trying to put a little scare into her, to make sure she didn't try that again. We both calmed down, and before she left, I took three twenty-dollar bills from my wallet and handed them to her. I don't remember why she needed the money and it really didn't matter to me. I had learned my lesson to keep my mouth shut, and it only cost me sixty bucks.

It was just a week or ten days later that I encountered Jesse again, this time at a party off in the woods. By the time I arrived, the action had already started. Since it was in an isolated opening back in the trees, parking was scarce, so I parked my truck about a quarter mile away and walked toward what appeared to be a giant bonfire. It was common to have a bonfire at these weekend parties, especially in the fall when the air is brisk and cool in the evenings.

I'm a likable guy, so as I walked up to the gathering I heard a few people should, "Hey, Erik!"

Locating a couple of friends, I reached into the bag of beers I brought and opened one up to start the evening. I knew how to drink, and I could hold my liquor. It was not really a party until I had downed at least a six-pack. The music was loud, the fire warm, the laughter steady, and everything was good.

But, it was about to get better. I spotted Jesse on the other side of the fire and began to think this might be one of those nights when I didn't go home alone. As I walked toward her, she spotted me and bounced my direction (and I mean bounced). She was dressed for a party, and it appeared she was glad to see me.

We drank and danced and laughed, and all the other dumb stuff people do when partying around a bonfire in the woods. As I said, I could handle my liquor so, in spite of already drinking a lot, I was still clearly aware of what was happening and what I was doing. I don't know if Jesse was trying to take advantage of what she thought might be my compromised state of mind, but she said she needed more money. This time she wanted a hundred bucks, and she pushed hard. In order to convince me that I needed to help, she threatened to tell everyone about me if I didn't pay up.

I put her off by telling her I didn't have any money on me and we would have to go to my apartment when we left. She seemed to accept that and turned her attention back to the festivities. On the inside, I was steaming. I had to make sure she didn't blab our little secret, and apparently my earlier threat wasn't enough for her. It was well into the morning hours when the party started shutting down and people began to leave. I put my arm around Jesse's shoulders, and we headed toward my truck.

I was accustomed to driving after drinking, so it was no problem for her to get in the car with me. I assured her that I would take her home after we got the money. We drove away headed in the direction toward town.

Jesse wasn't paying close attention, she had been drinking heavily also, so I turned off on a side road. She probably thought we were going somewhere private, and as I said, she was not averse to that.

I don't know when the thought of what I was going to do entered my mind, but I knew all along exactly what I was doing. There is no way I can blame it on the alcohol or being under any influence other than the need for survival. I don't know why she thought I could be blackmailed. Perhaps because I gave in so easily the first time, but I knew there was no stopping this path we were on and she would just keep demanding more and more money.

She viewed the information about me as leverage to allow her to get money whenever she wanted. I viewed the information as a threat to my life. It's not hard to tell which one of us was more motivated.

As we drove down the dark, tree-lined road, I made the car run rough, sputtering like it was out of gas. It was just a little trick caused by pushing on and off the gas pedal. I played it up big.

"Oh shit. I'm out of gas!"

Jesse didn't say anything. She didn't even act like she was concerned, I guess she assumed I was prepared to solve this problem. I was, but not in the way she ever suspected.

I pulled my track to the side of the narrow country road. There was no such thing as a shoulder, so it was still halfway on the pavement. There was no source of light other than what came from the vehicle. When you're that deep into the woods, even the light from a full moon is unable to penetrate. I stepped out of the truck and slowly walked around the back, thoughts of what I needed to do running through my mind. The gas tank opening was on the passenger side, so it was reasonable for me to come around to that side.

As I came around to the other side, I noticed a metal reflector post just lying on the ground. It was about five feet long and made a perfect weapon. I stood with my back to the truck and reached down to grab the reflector pole. When I opened the passenger door, I told Jesse I needed to get something. She backed away from me to give some space. As she slid across the seats, I struck her on the head with the pole in my hand.

It made solid contact, and she was obviously hurt. But, I didn't quit. I kept pounding and pounding, at least fifteen times. It was terrible.

Naturally, my mind wandered back to the experience with my grandfather. There were similarities. With him, there was blood everywhere. It splattered all over the room. With Jesse there was blood of course, but not all over the place. Probably because all the blows were confined to her head and she probably died after the second or third strike.

There was no doubt Jesse was dead. Now I needed to figure out what to do with her body. It's not easy to dispose of a corpse, which has been one of the biggest problems that keep murders from avoiding detection.

I tossed the blood covered pole in the back of the truck, and the slammed shut the passenger side door. As I walked around to the driver's side, I thought of the best idea I could come up with in the moment. We were close to a place called "Hell's Canyon." It's kind of a camper's and sightseer's mecca, but there are several ways out on trails that are seldom traveled. I took one of them and drove about five miles deep into the woods.

When I found a spot where I could park the truck, I stopped and got out to walk around to the other side of the vehicle. I knew there was no one watching, but I couldn't help but look around cautiously afraid someone might see me. When I pulled open the passenger's door, Jesse's body fell out and slumped up against me.

She was covered with blood, and her head looked like it had been through a meat grinder. I drug her body as deep into the woods as I could before totally being out of breath. I had no way to dig a grave or bury her, so I just left her there. I knew it would only be a matter of time before a hiker stumbled across her body.

I slowly drove home. I guess the stress and activity caused adrenaline to offset the effects of alcohol and I didn't feel the least bit drunk. The cab of my truck was splattered with blood, so I got a bucket of soap and water and some old rags to clean it out. I worked deep into the night cleaning up the mess. I knew there was no way to remove all the traces of blood, but I didn't worry about it.

I knew it wouldn't be long until the cops showed up and I would be arrested. Numerous people saw us together at the party, and I'm sure some of them even saw us drive off together. As soon as she was reported missing, the police would find me and solve the case. Especially once the body was found it would be obvious what I had done.

I had no doubt I would be going to prison. I knew how prison worked and how important it is to either have money when you go in or have someone on the outside taking care of you. Since I had no one who would take care of me, I began to stockpile as much money as I could. I did this the best way I knew—stealing.

I wasn't worried about Jesse and what I had done to her. I've thought about it, and I don't see any way that she could have really hurt me by talking. The people she would have told were just people like me. They weren't a threat. There was no rhyme or reason for what I did. I was simply in survival mode, and when anything that I perceived as a threat to that survival crossed my path, I overreacted. She didn't deserve what she got, but it happened, and there's nothing I can do about it now.

After a few months of building up my bank account and getting ready for prison, I began to believe nothing was going to happen. I never heard from anyone about Jesse. As far as I know today, they never found her body. I left it deep in the woods in an area that definitely has bears, wolves, and other carnivorous animals. I guess it's possible she was dragged off and eaten, which means she'll never be found.

The only hint of anything about the incident was a conversation I had with a State Trooper about eleven years later. He was asking some strange questions, and I sensed he was fishing for some answers, maybe trying to discern if I knew anything. However, that's never going to work with me. Years of experience with cops has taught me not to talk unless they're going to do something good for me. I have not been anywhere near that area in a long time, and have no plans to do anything to cause suspicion.

Once the realization that I was not a suspect in Jesse's disappearance, I decided it was time to move on. I could leave knowing the cops were not chasing me and the only person who knew I was hiding from bad guys out to kill me was dead.

Dysfunctional

There was an event that happened earlier, which I neglected to tell you about. At the time, it seemed about as significant as a pesky fly that is forgotten as soon as you wave a hand in its direction. While I was in prison, I was contacted by my father. Not my adoptive father, he never cared enough to make an effort, but by my birth father. He had family in the area where my mother lived, and somehow, he heard word that I was in prison. He didn't come to visit, but he did send a letter indicating he would like to see me some day.

I didn't respond, but I kept the letter. When you're in prison, you hang on to everything from the outside. It's a reminder that there is life outside of this hell hole. I had a small stack of letters that I kept bound by a rubber band, and my father's remained in that pile for several years. Those letters were always with me and in my possession through every change of address.

After a few weeks, I came to believe that I was not going to be a suspect in Jesse's death. I'm not even sure anyone knew that she was dead. I think I heard her name mentioned a half a dozen times at parties; people wondering, "Where's Jesse?" But, nobody seemed to care or even offered a guess. She might have been a runaway from someplace else; I didn't know. I kind of wish I had paid a little more attention when she talked about herself.

Once I felt like I might be in the clear, it was time to move on. I had been all over the area, and maybe a change of scenery would open up new opportunities. Where to go? I had no idea. I didn't know anyone who would want me showing up at their door-step.

One idea that did seem to have some possibility was my Dad. I still had the letter from prison, although I hadn't looked at it since the first day it arrived. I rifled through the stack of letters, found the one from him, and opened it to reread. Sure enough, there was an address and phone number where I could contact him.

I was hesitant to make a phone call, fearing that he might change his mind and tell me not to come. The best thing would be just to show up and surprise him. That would make it harder for him to turn me away. That's exactly what I did.

The address was in Colorado, a town I'd never heard of called Meeker. I knew it would be small enough that there would be no problem finding my Dad if he still lived there. Turns out it was easier than I thought. Like all small towns, as you enter via the highway, there was a row of billboards and signs advertising the various businesses in town. Most of them have been there for some time—missing a panel or held up by a rusted metal pole. I was shocked to see one of older faded signs for a trucking company bearing my Dad's name.

His shop wasn't on the main highway, but it was just a few blocks off and easy to locate. I drove up and parked, scouting the area for a few minutes. I watched men going in and out of the business and working around the yard. I had no idea what my Dad looked like. I guess I was just trying to find someone who looked like me.

I tired of the stakeout and decided to go inside and ask. As I entered the small office, a heavy-set man was wearing a faded red baseball cap giving instructions to a woman who was apparently the bookkeeper or secretary for the company. She was much better dressed as if she was the one who was expected to greet people when they entered the business. They both looked up at the same time, but with different expressions. The woman exuded warmth and interest as she asked if she could help. The man had a look of indifference like I was bothering him or taking some of his valuable time.

I responded to the woman's query by stating clearly why I was there. When I mentioned my father's name, the man stood up straight and gave me all of his attention. The woman turned sideways and took a step back as if to defer to him. The man asked, "What do you want?"

I identified myself and that I was looking for my father. The woman seemed a little puzzled because we don't share the same name, and I learned later that no one who knew my father knew anything about me. Dad was a little surprised, to say the least. He sized me up as if I was a new calf at a cattle auction.

He asked a few questions, and we talked back and forth for a few minutes—long enough for him to realize I was telling the truth. I didn't tell him everything that I had done since I got out of prison. There was no mention of drug running or living in hiding. It was going to take some time before we could develop any trust with one another.

Although Dad was convinced I was his son, explaining everything to his wife was going to take some doing. She was not happy about me being around. I stayed at the house while I was supposed to be looking for a job. However, job hunting has never been a skill I possessed. Hell, even keeping a job is not something I have ever done.

I didn't take long before the money I had was gone, and I was in need. Dad was away quite often driving trucks and his wife didn't like me hanging around the house. We seldom spoke to one another. I called Dad one day while he was on the road and asked if I could have some money. I needed some smokes and booze, but I was flat broke. He told me where to find his checkbook. He told me to write out a check for fifty-dollars and take it to a particular store and cash it.

I did just that. I didn't make the check out for any more than he instructed, just fifty dollars. At the store, even though it was evident I had signed the check, they wanted to verify my father approved it. They called the house, and his wife answered. When they explained that I was there trying to cash a check on my Dad's account, she didn't hesitate to tell them it was not authorized.

The next thing I knew the police were called. I was arrested for stealing from my own father and taken to the local jail. Although

I was quite comfortable being in jail, it was not the way I wanted to continue my life. When Dad got home and learned of the situation, he came to the police station and straightened things out. It was obvious that living at his house was not going to work.

I don't blame her. Few people would be comfortable having someone like me hanging around the house. She didn't like me, and I didn't like her either, so it was best that we parted ways.

I was able to enroll in a truck driving school a short distance away in Rawlings, Wyoming. Dad was doing well in the trucking business, and I watched him enough to know that I could do it well. First, I needed to get my CDL so I could legally drive large trucks. The course lasted five weeks, and I did well.

This is a good time to tell you that I was always a good student when I wanted to be. Reading was easy for me from the beginning, and I have a very rational thinking mind. If you could hear me speak you would be surprised how well I talk. I don't sound like an uneducated country bumpkin.

Neither do I look like someone who has spent such a huge portion of their life behind steel bars. My body is not covered with prison tattoos, and in spite of the numerous fights over the years, my face is not covered with scars. If I were to put on a suit and tie I could easily pass for a white-collar executive.

Truck driving school was easy. There was one huge difference between the other students and me. They were all hoping to graduate, get their license, and secure a job driving a big rig around the country. I had no desire to spend the rest of my life behind the wheel. The first thing I planned to do was buy a truck. The plan was to start my business on the first day.

Sure enough, with the ink still damp on my license, I went to a local truck dealership and identified a beautiful Peterbilt truck sitting on the lot. The salesman was eager to make the sale. I was ready to get my company started until he told me the price of the truck was two hundred thousand dollars.

It was obviously out of my price range, so he asked how much I could spend. I told him I had two thousand dollars and he almost hurt himself laughing. I worked hard to control myself because I don't like being laughed at, so I pressed him.

"Do you have anything closer to that amount?" I asked.

My inexperience was obvious and he did want to help, so he said, "Follow me son, let me show you what I can do."

We walked around to the back of their lot, passing several nice trucks I would have loved to own. It seemed that every time we passed one, the next was in worse condition. Finally, we arrived at the end of the lot, up next to a chain link fence, there was an old truck that was well past its prime. It was originally white, but the many dents had ample evidence of rust and dirt. He assured me that it ran, but I would have to take it "as is" because they would not warranty anything. I purchased my first truck that day, and my business was underway.

I hustled hard. I found jobs and drove countless hours. I never hesitated using substances to keep me awake so I could make more money. It didn't take long before I was in a position to purchase a better truck and secure more lucrative jobs. Things were finally looking up for my life.

It didn't last long before I became my own worst enemy again. I wasn't content being a working man just making a healthy living and staying out of trouble. I got involved with my Dad in a money-making scheme. We were moving loads from one truck to another and pretending to deliver for one customer, but in the meantime using the load to sell to another client. It was a complicated process that my Dad had devised, and I was the willing partner that he always needed.

We were doing so much stuff that it became impossible to keep everyone happy. You've seen those jugglers on TV who keep adding balls in the air. They move quickly past three, to four, to five, and perhaps even six before they stop. You know if they kept going there would be too many balls in the air, and they would start falling to the ground. That's the way we were with our trucking customers. We got caught.

We made about $50,000, and it was all in Dad's account. However, he got out ahead of me and ended up taking all the money and turning me over to the police. I was arrested after he made a deal. My attorney informed me that Dad was going to testify against me and I would have to pay back $19,000 in addition to going to jail. I was able to come up with the money and found myself back in prison.

Prison in Wyoming was essentially the same as everywhere else, except not quite as difficult. There was violence, but not nearly as bad as what I had encountered in other places. I would define it as easy time, and I got out after two years.

I didn't have any reason to stay in Wyoming, so I returned to Colorado. I didn't want to be in Meeker. Although my Dad had turned on me which resulted in prison time, we still had an on-again-off-again relationship. I didn't mind talking to him occasionally, but there was no way I was going to return to the same little town. The only other place I knew anything about was Grand Junction.

It was a larger town and also a place where I had no connections. I started from scratch, so I began by doing what I have always done best—I returned to alcohol. I was drunk constantly, but I was able to get a simple job at a deli. My manager was a woman named Jane. Since I was a little older than the other workers at the deli, she and I spent time together and we dated a little. She frequently reminded me that she didn't like my drinking, but she hung with me for a time. Then one day I passed out drunk at the gas pumps in front of the deli.

When I woke up and stumbled into the deli, she looked at me with disgust and said, "Fuck you!" and left completely—me and the job.

Since Jane was gone, the owner of the deli came in to run the place. Her name was Kim, and on the first day with her in charge of the shift, I stumbled into the store drinking a Red Bull.

Kim looked me in the eye and said, "Nobody cares what happens to you."

For some reason, her words cut through my stupid brain, and I took them to heart. I quit drinking. Just like that, I quit.

Kim was good for me at the time. Being sober allowed me to return to trucking and I once again developed a good business. I wasn't getting rich, but I was making a living. By this time, we were dating seriously. In fact, I even asked her father for permission to marry his daughter. He said yes, and we married.

At first, we lived in low-income housing in Grand Junction, but after some time, we were able to move to a place with an acre of land. We were happy, and things were good, but the thing about the trucking business, you can live anywhere you want. For some reason, my heart has always been in Oregon, so we talked about it for some time and eventually moved west.

Kim and I were married for six years. It was the most normal period of my entire life. We had two sons—James and Samuel. When you think about it, this life was far more than a person with my background could ever expect. Nobody would have ever thought I would be living the life of a typical husband and father, working a stable job and providing for a family.

It was too good to be true. Being an over the road truck driver, I would sometimes be gone from home for six to eight weeks at a time. It was more than I could handle and I cheated on her—often. When Kim found out, she wanted to be closer to family, so we all packed up and moved back to Colorado.

I guess I knew what she was doing and why she wanted to be with family. I was unwilling to fight for my marriage and family, so I went along with her plan. We barely got settled in Grand Junction before I was served with divorce papers. She gave it her best shot, but I was not going to change and be anything other than what I had always been. The only thing I ever cared about was me. Even with a wife and two boys, the only concern I had was what I wanted.

In my head, I know this is selfish and wrong. However, all my life, my survival has depended on me looking out for me alone. I have never felt secure enough that I could afford to waste energy and effort caring about someone else. Everyone in my life who was supposed to look out for me has turned their back and walked away from me. My birth father left shortly after I was born. My mother was mean and abusive. My adoptive father beat me incessantly. My grandfather sexually abused me and only quit because I killed him. My mentor Derrick. My girlfriend Jesse who threatened to expose me to those who would kill me. My real father who turned on me again about the trucking business.

I should have just walked away at that point. As a truck driver, I could live anywhere I wanted and built a good business. I didn't need to be near my wife and boys. They didn't want me around. There was no way we were going to have any kind of a relationship. But, once again, I chose the path that was most difficult for everyone. My relationship with Kim would take an ugly turn that nearly cost my life.

Smashed

I'll be the first to admit that I was not a good father to my two sons. Driving a truck, I was on the road and away from home constantly. A typical schedule would be two or three weeks away, two or three days at home, and then take off again. My sons were probably more comfortable when I was gone than when I was at home. But I didn't want to lose them.

When they came to deliver the divorce papers, there were about a dozen cops in the front yard. It was more like a military invasion than a simple divorce. I had no intention of contesting the divorce, but that wasn't good enough for Kim. She wanted to stick it to me as hard as she could, and I have to give her credit, she did. They made me leave the house with nothing but my wallet.

Not having anywhere else to go, I turned to my half-sister who lived in Meeker. I didn't know her well, other than the fact she was crazy. There was one time that she wanted to cook a hamburger for me. She put the meat in a skillet and had the flame turned up as high as possible and let it fry for an extra-long time. What she served was black and hard as a stone. When I told her I wasn't going to eat that shit, she reached over to my plate, picked up the meat patty, and hurled it at me like a baseball. It hit me square in the chest with an impact that left a scar that I still have to this day.

The only money I had in my wallet was in the form of Com Checks. This is a type of money used in the trucking business and they can be turned into cash. I asked my sister to run them through her bank so I could get the money. She deposited them, but a few days later she withdrew the money and I never saw it, more than $7,000.

Throughout the divorce process I turned to the one place where I could always find escape and comfort—alcohol. The drinking, combined with my long absences, made the decision of custody extremely easy for the judge. One other factor that I have failed to mention is that Kim's father was a cop. He had actually been County Sheriff for a couple of years but then lost an election and went back to work as a normal cop. He was, to say the least, influential in law enforcement matters in the county.

I tried to stay faithful to the every other weekend visitation opportunities I was afforded with the boys, although it was not always possible. However, when I did show up for the weekend, I was constantly pulled over and harassed by the cops. On one occasion they wouldn't allow me to remove my insurance card from my pocket, so I was arrested. I had to call my Dad who went to my house to get a copy of my insurance card to bring to the jail. They let me go, but that kind of stuff happened constantly.

Since I was unable to see my kids on designated weekends because of the police harassment, I stopped paying child support. It made sense to me. However, after a while, the state suspended by Driver's License for not paying child support. When I went to jail on that charge, I lost my trucking license.

I had to work, so I made a copy of the license of one of the drivers for my company. I put my photo over his and recopied it to make it look like my license. Sure enough, I was pulled over by the highway patrol for a violation, something that happens to truckers all the time. When he asked for my license, I told him that I lost it but I had a copy. I showed him the copy of the made-up license and there was no problem. However, when he asked me to sign for the ticket promising I would show up in court, my mind went numb for some reason, and I signed my name rather than the one on the license. Of course, I got caught, and went back to jail—this time for identity theft. I spent a year in prison and that is how my relationship with Kim and my sons ended.

When I was released from prison, I returned to my old stomping grounds in Colorado—where else was I going to go. I still wanted to see my boys and the only people I knew were in the area. Life was hard and I was struggling to figure out how to make things work. It seems like I was always starting over. I was in a bad routine. Things would go well for a while, then I would do something stupid, and everything would fall apart. I couldn't figure out how to break the cycle.

New Year's Eve came around and I didn't want to be by myself. Of course, I was drinking some at the time, but not nearly as much as in times past. I knew there would be people at the bar, which was better than sitting at home and drinking myself into a stupor. I was sitting at the bar minding my own business when my ex and her new boyfriend came in. They looked in my direction and I know they saw me, but they didn't say anything. Instead, they planted themselves in a booth right next to me. It was hard watching them act like teenage lovers. I know she was putting on a show for my benefit.

I didn't need to spend my New Year's Eve watching that, so I paid for my drink and left. It was close to eleven when I got home and I was pissed off. In fact, the later it got the angrier I got. Even though I had been drinking, I wasn't drunk. I knew exactly what I was doing.

I drove over to my Dad's house because I knew he wouldn't be home. The door was locked, so I kicked it open. I knew exactly what I wanted. I went to the bedroom where he kept a .357 in the closet. I grabbed the gun and a handful of bullets and stormed out of the house. Driving to Kim's house I knew what I needed to do. I was going to kill that fucker for messing with my wife.

By the time I arrived it was probably about two in the morning and I made sure her car was in the driveway. I grabbed the gun, walked up to the front door, and started pounding, demanding that they let me in. I was yelling obscenities and threats that could be heard all over the neighborhood. Inside, they were scared so Kim dialed 911. I was so loud they could even hear me on the phone.

She shouted through the door, "Go away, I've already called the cops and they're on the way!"

This really made me mad, so instead of pounding, I just kicked the door open and made my way inside. Kim jumped back and put down the phone, but she didn't disconnect the call, so the police dispatcher could hear everything that was going on. I ignored Kim and went over to grab her boyfriend, Tom George, by the throat. I forced him into a corner of the room and started spewing threat after threat to him. He was already scared before I took the gun and shoved the barrel into his mouth. I made sure he knew that I was going to kill him.

Tom fell to his knees and started begging me not to kill him. It was hard to understand his words which were being drowned by panic. I stood beside his quivering body with my hand on the back of his neck to make sure he didn't get up or try to run away. It took little effort to hold him down as he was too frightened to move. With my other hand I steadied the gun up against his head and reminded him over and over that he was going to die that night.

I didn't shoot him though. To this day, I still have no idea why I didn't kill him, but I didn't.

Now we were at a standoff. Tom was on his knees, shaking all over. I stood next to him, occasionally putting the gun next to his head just to remind him I could end his life at any moment. Kim stood over in another corner next to the phone, pleading with me to leave.

Outside the house was at least a dozen cops, including the SWAT team. The house was surrounded and there was no way I was leaving that night without someone dying. I didn't want it to be just me. The local cops were more than eager to take a shot as soon as one became available. They had wanted to get rid of me for a long time and this was their chance.

There was no escape plan. Obviously, I didn't think it through before kicking open the door. I was mad and I wanted to scare him and convince Kim to leave me alone, but there was no reason to kill him. To be honest, there was no reason for any of this to happen. It was such a waste of time. Like almost everything I had done, I was simply wasting my life once again.

Right in the middle of our standoff, my son came walking into the room. I hadn't thought about the boys being in the house. They must have been asleep upstairs and didn't hear the noise. As he came down the stairs and saw me with the gun pointed at Tom's head, he said, "Dad, what are you doing?"

It hit me right between the eyes. "What the hell am I doing?" I thought to myself.

I stepped back and pulled the gun away from Tom's head. I told Kim to tell the cops I'm coming out. She picked up the phone and spoke into the receiver. I could hear radio chatter from outside as the dispatcher relayed the information. As I walked toward the front door I laid the gun on a table next to the couch. I knew I didn't want to have that in my hand because it would definitely give them a reason to put a bullet in my head.

I felt like a whipped dog as I exited the house with my arms raised as high as I could raise them. In a loud, firm voice, I kept repeating, "I'm unarmed."

I tried to do everything the cops said with no sudden movements. There were cops everywhere. As soon as I stepped through the front door of Kim's house, two of them grabbed me and hurled me to the ground like a disgusting pile of garbage. I knew these guys were hoping for a chance to kill me and when I surrendered and walked out with hands raised, they lost the opportunity. They did the next best thing and beat the shit out of me. They dragged me over to the side of the garage to get out of sight of the crowd that had gathered in the front yard. It felt like every one of them got in a good punch or kick. I must have looked like a stubborn piñata at a kid's birthday party, everyone flailing away until I broke open.

I was sore all over, but my face seemed to take the worst beating. My nose was broken and several teeth were missing. My hair was soaked with my own blood. I still have a photo of my appearance when they booked me into jail. For the next three days I was left alone in a cell. There was no phone call or lawyer or visitors or even an arraignment. It seemed like the plan was just to leave me alone and let me rot by myself. It was beginning to feel I was going to live the rest of my life like a dog in a pen. I can remember thinking, "I'm done!"

On the third day, one of the guards came to the door and ordered me to put on my shorts. My face still looked terrible. My nose had been stuffed with cotton for three days to stop the bleeding and I was still bruised and sore. Every movement was a painful reminder of what had happened.

He led me to a room where a man was waiting to see me. Up to that point I had not been allowed to contact anyone, so I had no idea what this was all about. All I knew was that I was going to be charged with two accounts of kidnapping and assault and would live the remainder of my life in the pen.

The guard instructed me to sit at a table across from the man who was wearing an ill-fitting brown suit, and a tie that was not tightened all the way to the collar button. He was clean shaven, but his hair was scattered and somewhat longer than what you would expect to find on an attorney. Yes, he was a lawyer. He introduced himself, handed me a card, and then told me something that was going to change my entire situation.

There was a woman who lived a few doors down from Kim and her boyfriend. For some reason, I never learned exactly why, this woman hated the cops. It was probably an encounter of some kind with her family. Whatever it was, she hated the cops even more than me. She was awake on the night of the incident—it was New Year's Eve remember—and when she saw the commotion happening down the street, she put on her coat, grabbed a video camera, and ran down the street. When she arrived, little was happening, but she waited.

She was about to give up and leave when she noticed movement at the front door. She started up her camera and pointed it toward the house. She recorded everything. She had a video of me coming out with my hands in the arm. You could hear me screaming that I was unarmed, and it was obvious I did everything they instructed. Then you could see them pounce on me with a vengeance. She even had the sense to follow the action to the side of the house and continued taping the beating.

Instead of immediately taking the video to the police, she found a lawyer. She was as interested in sticking it to the copes as she was in helping me. Recognizing her chance, she found a lawyer. He was there at her request. When he told me all of this I wasn't sure what it meant. So what if the cops are in trouble—how does that help me?

The lawyer advised me to sit tight, not to say anything about it to anyone, and he would be back in touch in a couple of days. I knew how to keep my mouth shut in jail, and besides, I was pretty much confined to my solitary cell anyway.

It was four days before I was once again told by a guard to get dressed and follow him. This time he led me to a different place. It was not the meeting room in the jail, but an office in the police station next door. That same lawyer was at the table next to an empty chair where I was ordered to sit. On the other side of the table sat the Police Chief and another attorney.

My attorney did all the talking, as if he was in charge of things. He explained how I was facing indictments on two counts of kidnapping and assault and probably a few other lesser charges. With the evidence the police had there was no doubt I would be convicted and probably spend the rest of my life in prison. My first reaction to words from an attorney are usually, "That's bullshit," but I knew he was right.

He continued by explaining how there was a problem with the situation. He reminded me of the video tape. In fact, I was even allowed to look at the tape myself, and I've got to say, it's surprising I'm still alive. They beat me mercilessly. The garage was on the street corner and there was a stop sign in the background of the video. At one point in the video, I was tossed so high in the air that my face blocked the entire sign before plunging back to the ground for more blows. It was a gruesome sight.

The attorney then said that the video provided more than enough evidence to sue the Police Department, and the Sheriff's Office, and everyone else. He had no doubt I would win a large settlement and be financially set for life. However, he added that I would have to spend all the money at the prison commissary. But there was an alternative. He had worked out a settlement. The police would drop all charges against me and I would promise not to file a lawsuit. It was a win for both of us according to his words. I think both of us thought it was more like a loss, but everyone agreed.

I signed the agreement, charges were dropped, and I walked out of jail that afternoon as a free man once again. It was time for me to get out of Dodge, as they say. I gathered all my belongings, not much at this time in my life, loaded up the pickup and headed east. I had no idea where I was going, but any place was better than any place I had ever been before.

Demolished

I've been in jail or prison in seven different states. During the first 30 years of my life, at least a third of that time I lived behind bars. As I have recounted my story on the preceding pages, I have tried to be as honest as possible. I haven't described every crime I committed or stupid thing I have done, but there's no need—you get the picture. I have, however, described the most significant events without holding anything back. To be honest, this has been difficult for me because the information I have shared could come back to me and cause serious problems for the rest of my life.

But, there's one more event I need to tell you. It is the hardest of all to share, not because it's worse than the other stuff I did, but because I had no excuse. It should have never happened. It occurred when I was 30 years old. I wasn't a kid any more so I can't blame it on youthful stupidity. Like all my crimes, I had been drinking when it occurred, but I wasn't uncontrollably drunk. I knew the entire time what I was doing. It's unsolved by the police and if they put it all together, I could be in serious jeopardy.

I started out with the intention of writing a "tell-all" book and that is still what I have attempted. I am committed to telling it all, so here it is.

I was just 26 years old when Kim and I divorced. When I left Colorado, I searched for someplace where I would be accepted, or someone who would care about me. That's the story of my life. But, whenever I found what I was looking for, it never took long for me to destroy it all and have to start over in another place or with another person.

I made my way west, back to my roots. I don't know why I kept going there, but something seemed always to draw me back. I was still the same guy—drinking, stealing enough to get by, finding the parties, and just wasting my life. When I look back at my life and reflect, "What the fuck was I thinking?" I had wasted three decades on booze, drugs, and violence and had nothing to show for any of it. My life was a broken piece of shit.

The event I need to tell you about occurred at a party—of all places. And, as you have already surmised, I was drunk. I wasn't fall down drunk. With as much alcohol as I had consumed throughout my life, I seldom got so drunk that I was out of control. I was at this party with a girl. I need to tell you something about the girl or else you will want to ask a bunch of questions about what she was thinking.

I'm not going to tell you her name because there's no sense creating problems for her. This is my tell-all book, not hers. I know it's not nice to say, but the clearest way to describe this girl is that she was retarded. Her impairment wasn't blatantly obvious until you talked with her for a few minutes or watched how she acted in certain situations. She would make comments in the middle of a conversation that made no sense, or wander off for no reason at all. She was friendly and liked to party. She stayed with me throughout the evening without ever questioning what was going on because I'm not sure she understood. On top of her mental challenges, it didn't help that she spent the evening drinking and doing drugs.

The party took place at a cheap motel on the edge of town. The motel was constructed in a U shape, and in the center was a swimming pool and a couple of small buildings. The driveway circled the area containing the pool, and you could drive up and park in front of the individual rooms of the motel. It was one of those places for people who can't afford a good hotel.

There were at least 20 people at the party, in and out of the motel room and hanging out around the pool, although it was too cold for swimming. I don't even think the pool had any water. Like everyone else, I was drinking and having a good time. My problem often is that when I get a couple of Jack Daniels in me something bad is going to happen. This time was no exception.

A young kid, probably 20 years old, was being a nuisance all evening. He had a mouth on him that wouldn't quit and he just kept on and on and on. I walked outside to catch a smoke and stretch my legs. I walked to the end of the row of rooms where you could go through a corridor and get to the back of the motel. For some reason, this guy followed me wanting to talk.

It didn't take long before he and I were in a fist fight. I've already told you that I'm not big, which might be one of the reasons

I have had so many fights. Guys often think I'll be a push over. But, when I get in a fight, I never quit. I'm tenacious to the end. The only way you're ever going to beat me in a fight is to beat the shit out of me or kill me. The first has happened to me a few times, but obviously not the later.

The other guy was slender, and given the way he constantly ran his mouth, I'm sure this was not his first fight. There was just something about his voice, always yammering and talking nonsense that was aggravating. He was quick to the punch and landed the first solid blow of the fight. He got me square in the left eye with his right hand. I was stunned for a few seconds and the gushing blood and swollen tissue left me in a bad way. I couldn't see. He probably expected me to give up and walk away, but that's not me.

Being hurt only made me mad. Now I wasn't only fighting because of his obnoxious mouth, but also for my pride, and if I couldn't get the upper hand, maybe even my survival. Unable to see him or anything else, I just started swinging. Both of my hands were flying every direction and I could feel that I landed four solid blows to his face.

Although I still couldn't see well, I heard a thud sound and knew he must have fallen to the ground. I took a minute to wipe my eye with my shirt sleeve to clear away some of the blood. I was able to remove enough to survey the situation. He was lying on the ground, half way in a drainage gutter that encircled the entire front of the motel. As I said, when I'm in a fight, I don't quit. As soon as I saw him on the ground, I went crazy and started swinging my fists and hitting him as hard as possible.

Once I slowed down enough to realize he was unconscious, I stopped. For some reason, I felt like I needed to take one more shot. I dragged him up to the edge of the gutter and put his mouth on the curb. Then I raised my foot and stomped the back of his head as hard as I could. Obviously, his jaw was broken and he was in really bad shape. His mouth gaped open about six inches. I left him there and returned to the party.

This all happened pretty early in the evening so the party continued for a couple more hours. A few people began asking about this kid, but everyone just assumed he had left on his own. That seemed to be a clue for everyone else to leave so people started filing out of the motel room.

Although I was drunk, I still knew what I was doing; I was in control of myself. The girl and I hopped in my car, an ugly brown Toyota Celica with a loud muffler, the kind you hear coming from several blocks away. I backed out of the parking space and steered toward the location of our fight. I wanted to see if the kid was still there. I pulled the car to a stop, hopped out and walked over to where I left the guy. I don't know what I expected to find, perhaps hoping he had regained consciousness and went on home. I knew I had hurt him badly, but I had no idea how bad. When I got to the spot, I noticed, even in the blackness of the night, that his body was still lying in the same spot. I went over and grabbed his jacket and rolled him over, but as soon as I touched him it was obvious he was dead.

I knew I couldn't just leave him there. Once he was found in this spot, people would put it all together and implicate me. I rapidly walked back to the car to get the girl to help. The Celica had an unusual back end, kind of like a hatchback, but there wasn't a trunk. I opened the back and we struggled together to get the body inside the car. She knew what we were doing, but I never worried about her telling anyone. Between her metal disability and the drinking and drugs, it's likely she doesn't even remember.

Once we had the body in the car, I drove several miles out of town and dropped it on an old country road. It was another one of those incidents where I was confident I would be caught soon. They would find the body, make an identification, find out he had been at the party, and then learn that I had been there as well.

I didn't know this kid and he did nothing to me. I let his mouth get the best of me and lashed out. The result was that I took his life for no reason at all. He was not a threat to me in any way. The people I had killed before were a threat. My grandfather continually molested me sexually. Jesse threatened to expose me and get me hurt. But this kid did nothing.

I have no idea if they ever found his body. I assume they did. There was no reason for it to disappear from that country road. As far as I know, it's an unsolved murder. I don't know anything about it. I have never googled or called to get information. I'll never know.

Death

I know that last chapter ended rather abruptly, but that's precisely where Erik and I ended the conversation. That was on August 30th, three weeks and one day after our initial conversation. By that point I had already written the first five chapters and sent them to Erik.

He was overly excited when he received the first couple of chapters. He poured through them several times, making suggestions and notes and then sending them back to me for a rewrite. I was diligently working as quickly as I could because I knew he was sick and didn't expect to be around for long.

After the first couple of phone conversations, I had an outline in my mind as to how the story was to flow. At that point, each of our conversations focused on a specific chapter so that I essentially ended up with a recording to match each chapter of the book. It allowed me to keep everything together and make sure he told me everything he wanted me to know.

Erik was talking to publicists and working on book promotion in the meantime. He learned a great deal about the publishing industry and spoke to people I would never have been able to reach. He told of a phone conversation with a well-known publicist in New York. He talked her into reading the first chapter and she was impressed enough to call him and talk. When I asked how he did it, all he said was persistence. Apparently, she told him the next time he wanted to talk to her, create an interesting subject line for the email rather than send her 50 separate emails. He was persistent about getting what he wanted.

Because of his excitement, when I sent the fourth and fifth chapters, I expected to hear back within a day or so. However, a couple of days went by before he texted. He shared some crazy idea about deleting the first chapter and starting with the second. I asked for an explanation of his reasoning, but all he said was we'll talk tomorrow.

On September 2nd, I sent this message:

Erik, is everything ok. Haven't heard from you.

I got admitted yesterday around 5:30 I
will be released tomorrow Hopefully!!! I
have been working on chp 4

Two days later and I had not heard from Erik, so I texted once again:

Erik, how are things going? Call me?

Thirty minutes later I received this reply:

This is Kylie. They put him in a medical induced coma his liver is in full distress. They are getting his transplant all put together should happen Friday. I've got to get back I will keep you updated.

Kylie is Erik's wife. We had never talked, but he had talked about her often. I also know that he had told her a lot about me. This news hit me hard. It was completely unexpected. The last time I heard from him he anticipated being out of the hospital the next morning and we had plans to continue on the book. I didn't know what to say, so I meekly replied with one word— "OK."

But Kylie had something to say:

Thank you for checking on him. He does not have many people who could care less. He is a great guy if he cares. Not many get to see that!

I don't know how much it means to you guys, but I'm praying for you and I really do care.

It means a lot. He cares a lot about
you, did he tell you he got in a fist fight
because someone criticized your writing.
He is loyal as a pit bull if he likes you

When I read this text, I remembered a conversation Erik and I a week or so earlier. He mentioned that someone criticized his story and it made him mad. I told him that if was going to be a writer he needed to learn how to handle criticism—it comes with the territory. He indicated he would work on it, but he said nothing about getting into a fracas.

I knew he would be in a medically induced coma until after the surgery, but three days later I texted just to check in. She replied that there was no change and it was simply a matter of waiting until Friday for the surgery. She told me that surgery was scheduled for 10:30 and I reminded her we would continue to pray.

Thank you so much. I need him to make it through.

I understand.

No you don't he is my SOUL I can't
live without him. This man would walk
through hells fire for me I want to do that
for him now
I sit at his bed stroking his hair. They know
visiting hrs do not apply they want me out

bring the army Cuz it's gonna take all of them
Anyway got to get back tomorrow is going to be really hard for me

I waited all day Friday but didn't hear anything. Finally, at 8:00 pm I asked if she had heard anything.

He just got out of surgery he is in recovery now

Great news. It's been a long day. We are so glad to hear. We have been praying all day

I really meant that. I prayed for Erik all day long. I was truly worried. Sharon was confident he would be fine, but I was struggling. I don't know why it was so difficult for me. I only knew him for about a month and we never met face to face. If you handed me pictures of two men and asked which one was Erik, I would have a fifty-fifty chance of picking the correct one. But for some reason I felt close to him. I had a lot of thinking to do about that.

A little before noon the next day I asked if Erik was awake yet.

He was for about 2 hrs they are putting him back under til Thursday take stress off

Were you able to talk to him?

Yes and give him a couple of kisses.

Kylie sounded to be doing well, hopeful that he was going to be ok. She told me he was mad because she had shaved his head. I couple of days later I received this text:

He is awake Dr says he looks good
His body seems to be accepting it well

On Friday, just before 10:00 I received this text:

Hey hey hey

Is that you?

Yes sir. Sorry I've been out of contact for a bit

I've really been concerned.

No need for concern I will be 100 percent in a month or so
Well maybe not 100 but enough to whip an ass or 2
Like 5 million dollars in a 1 million dollar sack

Broken

Dr says I've got to do a lot of resting for a

bit

Sorry I didn't text before surgery I was a

Lil preoccupied

You've been unconscious for two weeks so it will take some time.

I want you to know that it means a lot that you checked on Kylie

I care about you guys

Did Kylie tell you she bought a farm in ND while I was getting taken care of. And she shaved by f___ING head

She told me she was going to shave your head and that you would be mad. She didn't say anything about the farm

10 acres

Congratulations on the farm. How long do you think it will be until we can get back to work?

I'll be ready in 1 week

That conversation took place on Saturday and Monday I asked how he was doing.

Getting better sore but I feel pretty good

Is your liver functioning well?

Yes my body is accepting it well

Great – you're going to exceed the 60% they estimated.

My last comment reflected the results of a medical test he took several weeks prior to the transplant surgery. They told him then that he had a 60% chance of survival with a transplant.

Dr says my prognosis looks good. I might be released Thursday

You've made it through a rough patch. You'll get stronger every day from now on. I'm so glad to hear this.

I can't wait to get out of here

You've slept through most of it.

But the part I've been up for is making me
nuts.

On Wednesday, I had not heard anything from either even though I had texted Erik a couple of times. In the early afternoon I asked Kylie how he was doing. Her reply caught me totally unprepared.

I can't explain right this minute but his
body had a reaction to something he
passed on Tuesday morning at about 3 am
I can't talk right this minute I am in the
funeral home

You mean he died?

I will call you a little later
Will you write his memorial?

And with those words, Erik was out of my life. Well, that's not exactly correct. He died, but he was far from out of my life. This was not something I could just walk away from and forget. The story is too powerful and our compacted relationship was too intense to allow me to quit.

But, that explains why his story ended so abruptly. His life ended just as abruptly.

But Erik wasn't out of my life, not really. There is something about him that has stuck with me and has caused me to grieve his death more than most.

The original plan was for him to tell the story up until the time he and Kylie met. At that point she would relate the story from her perspective. I'm not sure that would have ever happened, because apparently, she doesn't like to talk on the phone. In fact, I've never heard her voice. I would love for her to finish the story. She has promised that she will but needs some time to process everything. However, she plans to return to her home in England so I'll be surprised if I ever hear from her.

The texts we shared after Erik's death indicate she is quite angry. It is the expected anger of a grief process and it is exclusively directed at him for leaving her after he had promised he would make it through the surgery. I know she needs some time, but I fear that she doesn't have anyone to help her resolve her issues. She is also angry about the book because it took so much of Erik's attention that he could have given to her during his final month.

There was one day early in the process when Erik texted me and said he was quitting, there was not going to be a book. I called him to ask what was going on and he said Kylie got mad about some of the things he had shared. It seems that she didn't know all his background, although I do think she knew what kind of man he was. They fought about the book, and when he got up the next morning she had left.

I haven't told you yet that he and Kylie have two young children, toddlers who require time and attention. Erik planned to spend the day finding a Nanny he could trust. He was also upset and bitter and used the phrase "good riddance" when describing Kylie's departure.

I can understand his anger, and I can understand her's as well. They were facing an impossible situation. They were living in a tiny apartment that was attached to a motel. They had only been there a short time and much of that time was spent with Erik in the hospital. He was facing the prognosis of death in six months according to the doctor's estimate. Erik told me that he thought it would be more like five. They had two young children and no family or friends. The only person who seemed the least bit interested in them at the moment was me, and we had never met face to face.

I understand why she left Erik, although it's incomprehensible that she left her children. I know the stress was overwhelming, but really! Late that evening I called Erik just to see how he was doing. I could tell that things were better as soon as I heard his voice. He said that Kylie had returned after several hours and they had worked things out. He was ready to get back to work on the book.

We talked again about Kylie providing the information for the last part of the book via recording. He assured me that she was excited to be a part of the book and she could tell about their life together better than he could. She still might once she works through her anger, I won't be surprised either way.

I never received any specifics about writing a memorial so I don't know how that was handled. She was angry that he had to be cremated for some reason. She said he didn't want that. He always said he should just be stuffed in a box and packed away in an old closet when he died. She did promise to stay in touch with me.

I'm not mourning the loss of the book. Although, I will admit, it's a powerful story that could make a great movie someday. Erik talked about that possibility often. He said that no matter how successful the story became; he and I were partners. He got 60% and then 40% for me. I have no doubt he would have remained true to that promise. He genuinely liked how the story was shaping up. I admit, the prospect of a story I wrote becoming a best-seller and perhaps even a movie is exciting. But my mourning is not about losing that. The truth is, the story is still there. You've already read much of it, and there are enough smatterings about the rest of his life scattered on the recordings that along with a good imagination I could finish the entire thing.

Before I move on, I do need to say something about the story itself. As Erik's story unfolds it is missing a key element. There is no resolution to the crisis. Every good story has a crisis; that's what the story is all about. It might be a murder to solve, a relationship that needs to be restored, a mystery to explain, or something that takes up the final pages of the story. When you put the book down you need to feel like the story is complete. There might still be loose threads, but the main issue has been resolved.

However, this story has no resolution. It is the tale of a man whose entire life is characterized by violence and drugs. Even if I wrote the rest of the story, it would end just like the last chapter ended—something terrible happened and he just kept going. I needed to create an ending that had no basis in reality, but that would defeat the purpose of writing a "tell-all" book. I felt like I was riding a wild horse and had no way of getting off without dying.

If I do create a fictitious ending, what would it be. It seems disingenuous to have a "they all lived happily ever after" type of thing. There was nothing in Erik's life to indicate he might find happiness. He did seem happy with his marriage and two children, but he was also living with a medical death sentence at age 39, and having to live under a false identity for fear of being located by people who will kill him. How do I resolve all of that without writing some far-fetched saga?

There is also the question about the likability of the main character. How can I write a story where the protagonist is an unrepentant murderer who spent the most productive years of his life smugglings drugs across the border from South America? I talked about this with Erik and he completely understood the dilemma. I told him that I was going to try and make him a "sympathetic" protagonist of the story. What I mean by that is present him in such a way that people will understand him and have sympathy for him, even when he does bad things.

One of the best examples I can recall of such a character is Walter White from the TV show *Breaking Bad*. He continually went from doing one bad thing to another throughout the entire lifetime of the series. However, we felt sympathy for him because we understood why he made such choices.

There's a valuable lesson about life found within this concept of a sympathetic protagonist. All of us have made bad choices. In fact, many have made terrible choices that have turned out damaging, or even fatal, for others. In might be correct to say that we are all sympathetic protagonists of our own story. However, in Erik's case, it is important to explain the reasons for sympathy clearly.

That takes me to the title we chose. Within the first week, Erik and Kylie started throwing title suggestions my way. I've written and published numerous books for others and some people have a definite title chosen before they ever talk to me, and others have no idea and instruct me to pick one for them. Usually we work together to come up with something appropriate.

They quickly narrowed it down to "Broken Roads." I like it, but I thought we could do better. However, they ran with it and created a cover concept and began work on a website. I tried to keep the conversation open. Once I began working on the manuscript the title we needed was clear. There was nothing to suggest a "road" other than a synonym for "life." However, I really liked the simpler, "Broken." When I explained my reasoning to Erik, he talked to Kylie, and they both liked it better as well.

Here's my reasoning: Erik was broken from the beginning. He was born into a violent family. He was physically and verbally abused by both parents and his siblings for as long as he could remember. When he was removed from that situation, he was given to live with his grandparents where he was continually sexually molested. From there he began his prison journey because of his first murder. Everything else that happened for the remainder of his life caused the damage to get worse and worse.

Everything about his life was broken—his choices, his relationships, his circumstances. I'm not talking about a Calvinistic doctrine of the total depravity of all men. His life was broken by forces beyond his control. That is certainly not to excuse the things he did. In fact, Erik said several times that people didn't deserve what he did to them. But to try and understand why someone acts the way they do does not mean we must excuse their actions.

My father was always a Buick man. I don't know how he got to be that way. He probably bought one that turned out to be a good car, which led him to buy another, and soon he was hooked. For most of my life he only bought Buicks. One year when he went to trade in his used car for a new Buick, the dealership did not have the one he wanted. However, they had an Oldsmobile that was identical to the Buick he wanted. Back in those days, the only difference between the two brands was a couple of design alterations.

The salesman convinced my father to buy the Oldsmobile, even gave him a good price. From the start, that car was a lemon. Stuff quit working and there was one problem after another. It seemed like the car was in the shop more than on the road. It didn't take long for Daddy to get frustrated and return the car to the dealer and get another Buick. From that moment on, no one dared mention the word "Oldsmobile" in our home again.

That Oldsmobile was like Erik. There was something wrong with it from the beginning and nothing short of a miracle was going to fix it. Once we determine that something is broken and beyond repair, we cast it aside. Just like my Dad turned his back on all Oldsmobiles from that day forward, we frequently do the same thing with people like Erik. For many people, he can never be a sympathetic protagonist.

The title "Broken" became more and more important to me as I learned the full extent of Erik's story. Everything about him was broken. Do you remember the story from his childhood when he stole the toy and gave it to the boy in the wheelchair? He said it was the last time he ever felt good about anything. Imagine that. What if the last time you felt good about anything in life was when you were nine years old?

When Erik told the story about how he killed his grandfather, it was a somber moment for both of us. It was difficult for him to relive the experience and it was difficult for me to hear it for the first time. I thought about it that night. The next time we spoke, I made a point to tell him that I understood something about killing his grandfather. Erik was a year younger than my oldest son, and I caught myself speaking to him at times like a father. I think he even came to accept and appreciate that.

I told him that if my son were being sexually abused repeatedly, by his grandfather or by anybody, I would have no problem if he took matters into his own hands and killed him. I know that sounds harsh and I'm certainly not advocating the death sentence for child molesters, but as a father, I understand. I would certainly be angry with myself for not doing something sooner to solve the problem, but I would stand by my son. I suspect I was the first person ever to tell Erik that his act was understandable. Remember, his own mother rejected him and even supported the strongest possible sentence by the court.

I hurt when Erik told me that story. I could feel the pain in him although he never said he felt sorry or wished he hadn't done it. The reason this experience and the others he would share down the road were so emotional to me is because I understood that he was broken. Everything about him and his life was broken. All the people in his life were broken. It is not surprising that he made such terrible choices and committed painful actions. He was broken.

When you understand how broken Erik was, it takes a cold-hearted person to not have some sympathy for him. Many years ago, I heard a woman who had spent her life working with children say, "There's no such thing as a bad kid; there are only misguided kids." She was pointing out that there are reasons we act the way we do. Certainly, we are responsible for our sins and mistakes, but that doesn't mean that other factors are not also involved. When I hear Erik's story, he becomes a very sympathetic character.

But that's not all. He said something to me in one of our early conversations that stuck with me and after his death it forced me to dig deeper into what he might have meant. I think it will do the same thing for you.

Memorial

"My grandmother always told me that she believed I was an angel from heaven. I never really believed it, but when you look back, I should be dead, more than dead. I should be in prison, but I'm not. I don't know if God really had something, and I was too stupid to ever follow it or what, but my Grandmother was convinced God had some huge plan I was supposed to fill, and then she died, and I messed it all up and who would ever use me for anything..."

These words are a direct quote from Erik. It's a vivid memory that he spoke about two times in our conversations. It's apparent to me that he had given his grandmother's opinion some thought and came to reject it as pure nonsense, but I haven't been able to let it go that easily.

If you think back to Erik's introduction of his grandmother into the story, you will remember that she was not a gentle, matronly woman that the word "grandmother" often conjures in our mind. She was a hard-working, hard-driving woman who shocked him with an over-familiarity with death. Remember how she killed a cow he loved without warning right in front of him. She also remained silent for the two years that his grandfather sexually assaulted him at night.

Obviously, I don't consider his grandmother as any kind of prophet or spokeswoman for God. She was not the kind of woman we should turn to for spiritual guidance. However, there was some reason Erik remembered the words quoted above. The idea that God had something special for Erik would not go away even after learning about the horribly unproductive life he lived.

I am well aware that God frequently uses broken people to accomplish great things. The first one who comes to mind is Samson. Samson had squandered the blessings God had given him out of lust for a woman. He gave everything away because he couldn't say no to temptation. Yet, even after his enemies captured him, blinded him, and chained him up for mockery and ridicule, God used him in a way that causes us to retell his story. There was nothing in Samson's life that would indicate he could be employed by God.

Numerous biblical characters were broken by life. What about Moses who was set adrift in the river as an infant, or Isaac lain out on an altar staring at his father's hand with a knife set to plunge into his heart, or David who was such an inconsequential person to his father that he wasn't considered worthy of meeting God's prophet. Do you see what I mean? None of us make it through life unbroken.

The difference between most of us and Erik is that even though we were broken at some point, we had someone in our life who came along and mended us. Such was not the case with Erik. He went from one abusive situation to another. It would have been like my father taking his Oldsmobile to the junkyard instead of the mechanic, and while at the junkyard, people kept coming along and taking all the parts. Erik never left the junkyard. He was continually broken and had no opportunity for repair.

At this point, let me explain my personal opinion of Erik. As I've already stated, I only knew him for barely more than a month and never met him face to face. We spent many hours talking on the phone, and I've listened to those conversations over and over. However, I'm confident that at the time of his death, Kylie might have been the only person who knew him better. As we waded through his life story, he never once mentioned anyone who was ever a friend. He never spoke of a person who cared about him for anything other than what they could get from him. I suspect that's why he liked me as well as he did. I truly cared for him, and he knew that.

My first impression of Erik, before I heard his story, was that he put his life together and was a success at something. He had money, he was well-spoken. In fact, one day I even asked him where he was educated. He had a good command of the English language, spoke without any type of regional brogue, and used little slang. He was educated in prison is what he told me. He didn't have many classroom opportunities in his life, but he said the teachers he did have typically told him he was a good learner. He also indicated that he liked to read, which might be the best way for anyone to get a good education.

I do know that when he became interested in a subject, he was tenacious to learn as much as fast as possible. He peppered me with questions about book marketing and publishing. Within a week, he knew more than I do about publicists and agents. He spoke to several and piqued their interest in our project. He convinced a well-known publicist to read the first chapter of the book, something that many authors are unable to do in years of trying.

There was a simple kindness about Erik that you sometimes see in young children. During our first few conversations, he continually apologized for things. He would frequently say, "I'm sorry..." and then proceed to tell me something, even when he had done nothing wrong. After a while, I just flat out told him to quit apologizing. "You need to stop saying I'm sorry all the time," I said. "When you've done something wrong that's fine, but otherwise, I don't want to hear it." Of course, he apologized, but then he quit.

He was also willing to learn. I could tell he was serious most of the time, I told him that one of the three things about life that I know for sure is that people need to laugh more. (I planned to discuss the other two with him at some point, but it never happened.) He said that he would work on it. A few days later he told me that he was playing on the floor with his children and Kylie said there was something different about him. She affirmed that normally when he played with the children, he would be distracted, not really enjoying the time. However, on this particular occasion, he was sincerely laughing and having fun. He then thanked me for telling him to laugh more.

Erik lived the last decade of his life in hiding from people who were anxious to kill him. He had learned how to change his identity and practice deception. He explained how he changed his identity. It involved applying for and obtaining a Notary Public designation and then using that to get a new birth certificate. It was a complicated process that I never fully understood. He told me that his new identity was so secure that he was even able to travel back and forth across the border to Canada without detection.

Knowing that he was so adept at deception, I was continually aware that the story he was telling me might be total fiction. I listened to indications that he was making things up. I'm certainly not a specialist in detecting lies, but I can say that when he told the same story multiple times, the details remained consistent. He never made himself out to be the hero of an experience as you might expect from someone who is lying.

The one thing I struggled with was his current location. During our month together, he traveled some and not all his travel plans made sense. However, in the end, when I look back over things, I think it was more of a miscommunication than deception. The one time I asked him where he was at the moment, he told me and provided a description of the town and place where they were staying. It was the same town Kylie identified as where she was when he died, so I think he was honest when I asked.

At one point he even told me his real name. That is the one thing I'm not sure about concerning his honesty. The only reason is because of the strange coincidences surrounding that name. It would truly be odd if it is his real name, although it might explain some other things. (I'm not going to tell you, so let your imagination run wild.) It didn't matter to me at that point. I was flattered that he was willing to reveal his true identity to me, even though I didn't ask. I was always careful not to be pushy about sensitive information. I know he gave fake names for victims and other characters. Sometimes it was to protect others and sometimes it was to protect himself. On one of the recordings, when I listen carefully, I note that he slipped once when talking about Derrick and used a different name. He quickly caught himself and corrected it.

There was never any reason for him to lie about anything to me. If he did make up the whole thing he has a great imagination and he's an idiot for making himself out to be such an evil man. I have no doubt the story is true, perhaps embellished a bit like all of us do when we tell stories of our past.

At one point, I asked Erik if he thought he would ever kill anyone again. Without hesitation, he replied that it was something in his past and that it would never happen again. He really felt like he had changed. If you look back over the three times he killed someone, it was either a moment of survival or rage. None of them were premeditated. He was convinced he had moved past that flaw in his personality.

However, about a week later he had an occasion to call his mother on the phone. He was trying to secure some old photos that he might want to put in the book, so even though he hadn't spoken to her in years, he thought he would ask. It came about after a long-convoluted process where he posed as a private investigator working for his son and an elaborate made up story. In the end, while on the phone, he identified himself to his mother and she cussed him out and called him all kinds of unimaginable names. When Erik told me about the incident, he said, "You remember when I told you I would never kill anyone again? I was wrong."

In that moment, he realized he still had a problem with rage. It was caused by the one person in his life who should have been loving and supportive—his mother. This was the final contact they ever had with one another, and it ended in bitterness and anger. He was still broken, and the one who first broke him was the culprit.

I told a few people about the project, and several of them asked if I was afraid he might want to kill me some day. To be honest, I never thought about it or had a moment's concern. About halfway through the process, Erik told me that he and Kylie were planning a trip back west soon and planned to stop in Fort Worth to meet me in person. I thought it was a great idea and I was even willing to let them stay at our house. I'm not sure if all of my family would have been comfortable with that idea.

There is one final issue with the whole experience I want to resolve. I need to know what this whole thing was about. Why did it happen? Why was I a part of the process? What can I learn?

I don't believe in coincidences. I am convinced that God brings people into our lives for a reason, and I pray every day for an opportunity to make a difference in someone's life. Erik finding me was not an accident nor a coincidence. Now I'm struggling to figure out the purpose.

Somewhere buried deep in his memory bank was his grandmother's notion that God had a plan for his life. Then he came to me to write his story. I asked him why he chose me because I know he had other options. He said he had looked at my website and read some of my stuff and liked what he discovered. You don't have to see very much of what I have written to realize most of it is from a Christian perspective. I have been quite open through my writing about my faith. I would think that my religious background and experience would turn away someone like Erik, but it didn't. There must be a reason that goes beyond him simply liking my style.

I'm positive of some things this experience was NOT about. It was not about Erik, or someone like him, "finding Jesus." I'm not saying that would not be great. I won't even deny that I prayed that he would find the spiritual life that only Jesus provides. But I don't think that was the purpose of our encounter. Erik was not attracted to me because he was seeking salvation. He was not looking for a "holy man" to restore his soul. There was not one moment when I felt like he had an interest in spiritual matters.

As often as Erik had been locked up, I'm confident he had heard the Gospel several times. Christians are quite active in prison ministries, and many inmates are vocal in sharing their faith with other inmates. Not only were their much better and easier options if this was about hearing the Gospel, but also, I never sensed any type of leaning or encouragement to bring it up with Erik. If God was leading him to me for that purpose, He should have at least given me a head's up.

I not saying I had no intention of sharing the Gospel with Erik at some point. I did. In fact, I told Sharon that someday Erik and I were going to have a "come to Jesus" conversation. I knew the time wasn't right now, but it would be eventually, but it never arrived. Even through all my grief over Erik's death, I never felt guilt or remorse for not breaking out the *Four Spiritual Laws* or leading him down the *Roman Road*.

The closest I came was the day I shared with him about three things I know for certain. The only one of the three that I mentioned to him as that people need to laugh more. The other two are life is hard, and God is good. He already knew that life is hard and I was convinced he was not ready to hear me saying that God is good. He wasn't ready to hear that message. I hoped he would be someday, but that was not the purpose of my adventure with Erik.

Nor do I think the purpose was for someone to have the opportunity to convince Erik he was a bad person. He already knew that. He knew more than anyone that much of the stuff he had done was wrong, and he mentioned several times that people he harmed didn't deserve what happened to them. I'm confident Erik didn't tell me everything he had done because it defied explanation. There was one episode he described to me, but the next day he asked me to not use it. It was bad enough in his mind that he didn't want Kylie to know.

I believe the purpose of the relationship between Erik and me was not for any of the above reasons, but I don't mean to suggest that there was not a spiritual purpose. There are several spiritual truths found in his story that will be meaningful to me the rest of my life, and I hope they resonate with everyone who reads Erik's story.

I gained a much better understanding of what it means to be a broken person. At the very outset of this book, I talked about broken people being attracted to me for some reason. I have known many of them over the years, but Erik was by far the most broken person I have ever known.

I don't feel qualified (nor interested) to debate the theological doctrine of total depravity. I get that every one of us finds a way to do bad things in spite of the best of circumstances. However, most of us have enough good circumstances to give us a fighting chance to be a good, decent person. I was born into a stable family with two parents who loved and nurtured me from the day I was born until they were no longer able. Even now as my mother struggles with dementia, whenever I'm around she worries about me rolling off a curb in my wheelchair. I was blessed with that kind of environment all my life.

Whenever my broken parts reared their ugliness, my parents helped me put things back together and experience healing of my soul. Many other people have come in and out of my life to help smooth over the rough parts of me. Whenever I have been broken, someone has always been there to put me back together.

The same is true for most of us to some extent. You might not have been quite as fortunate as me, but you probably had folks who cared for you and tried to steer you in the right direction; people who would put you back together and kept you from being tossed on the scrap heap. Without these people, we would be useless.

Erik didn't have anyone like this in his life. From birth, he was an inconvenience to his mother, forcing her to endure an extra month of pregnancy because he wouldn't come out. His stepfather hated him and began to beat him at an early age. Even his siblings took every opportunity to make life difficult for Erik.

As he grew up, he never found that person who would be able to help him. The closest thing he ever had was his friend Derrick who was merely grooming him to be a part of his drug business. In the end, Derrick and his skinhead brothers are the ones who would be more than happy to kill Erik. His first wife, Kim, might have tried, but she turned on him quickly and allowed her cop father to make his life miserable.

A couple of years ago he met Kylie. I don't know much about that relationship. I have no idea how they met. I'm waiting for her to contact me and finish that part of the story. She has been a positive influence, but even her love appears to be conditional at times. She left him during the time he was working on his story with me—left him with their two young children. Several times he mentioned that she held certain things over his head threatening to leave him if he did the wrong thing. He loved her, and she loved him, but I'm not sure she was any less broken. He told me that she had come here from England, where she left two kids behind to get away from something. Again, a story I have not yet heard.

Are some people broken beyond repair? I don't know. It's hard to imagine anyone being more broken than Erik, yet I think there was still the opportunity for repair for him. It might be that time ran out for him at age 39, but I think he was still seeking and I know that I was willing to help in any way possible. He chose to spend the final part of his life telling his story. Was he still looking for someone to accept him?

During my short relationship with Erik, I learned a great deal about loving the unlovable. Some of the things he told me were hard to hear, but I made a deliberate decision at the beginning that I was not going to judge him or offer my assessment of his life. Instead, I chose to love him to the best of my ability. I was determined to be non-judgmental.

One of the most valuable lessons I have learned in my life is that it is not my job to judge another person or the way they live. That work belongs to God. If God wants to condemn someone, He doesn't need my help. All I have been asked to do is love them. Some people read the Bible and focus on Jesus' condemnation of sin, and the harsh judgments of God described in the Old Testament. Jesus might have condemned sin, and God might have been harsh at times, but that responsibility was never passed on to me. My goal with Erik was to convince him that someone loved him and that eventually that would open the door for him to see that God loves him as well. Unfortunately, death came before I got to see that happen.

A friend suggested that Erik's story was a confession. That might explain why he turned to me, a religious man, perhaps seeking absolution for his sins. That idea resonates with me on several levels. His story was an extended confession of sorts. There was never a hint of pride in what he had done or bragging about his accomplishments. On the other hand, there were few expressions of contrition or sorrow for what he had done.

I don't know if he was seeking forgiveness or absolution. If he was, I'm afraid he died too soon. By the way, he knew he was dying, but he thought he had more than six weeks. He told me that doctors said it would take six months, but he felt he wouldn't be around quite that long, perhaps four or five. If he could have lasted another month or two, he might have been able to realize absolution and forgiveness from God.

When Erik died, I could have simply walked away from the story and quit the writing process. It was, after all, his story, not mine. However, I couldn't do that because his story had actually become my story. The experiences he related were so out of the ordinary for me that I spent a lot of time reflecting on what this whole thing was about. I invested heavily in trying to understand Erik, and I couldn't simply leave him once he took his final breath.

Erik had been given a death sentence—not by a judge but by a doctor. Once that happened, all he wanted to do was tell his story in his words. As he said at the outset, he wanted to write a "tell-all" book. I've tried my best to make that happen. We didn't tell it all, but I think we told enough for you to understand him. Hopefully, I've told it in such a way that you recognize a sympathetic protagonist.

I plan to keep the recordings and play them occasionally, at least the first part of every conversation that always went the same. The phone rings and Erik answers. I say, "Hi Erik."

He replies, "Hey young man, how 'ya doing?"

He always sounded happy to hear my voice, and he always called me "young man" even though he knew I was old enough to be his father. My biggest regret in our entire relationship is that he died before I could introduce him to my heavenly Father.

www.ingramcontent.com/pod-product-compliance
Lightning Source LLC
LaVergne TN
LVHW011233080426
835509LV00005B/470